SEÁN Ó RIADA
HIS LIFE AND WORK

Tomás Ó Canainn, from Derry, has lived in Cork for many years
and was Dean of Engineering at University College Cork.
When Seán died in 1971, Tomás succeeded him in the Music Department
and combined two very diverse disciplines.
Joint author of a biography in Irish of Ó Riada and musical editor
of two of Ó Riada's publications, Tomás was also a founder member
of Na Filí, a world-famous Irish traditional group.

Homo Ludens

And he told this story
of the old singer and the tape recorder:
of how the old man listened to his own voice
while fierce anxiety turned down his mouth
until he heard his strengthening voice
move into life again.
Then sat with concentration till the song was over,
flung his cap on the floor between his boots crying,
   'I'll never die!'
Another night Seán sat down at the piano
when we were drinking poitín and pints of stout
and played the tune to me for the first time,
that air of pride and loss,
of the sharp love that has accepted loss.
And in his hands our deadly lasting sadness
became acceptable
so I was moved to tears,
not drunk but steady.
I cried,
and when he finished cursed him saying, 'You bastard,
you took me by surprise'.
He stood up with his fingers round my arm
smiling and laughing;
pleased with my understanding,
more pleased by his power,
most deeply pleased by music
   by the thing itself.

One afternoon he said,
'A man should dance on his own floor'.

And he danced.

Seán Lucy

SEÁN Ó RIADA
HIS LIFE AND WORK

TOMÁS Ó CANAINN

The Collins Press

Published in 2003 by
The Collins Press
West Link Park
Doughcloyne
Wilton
Cork

British Library in Cataloguing in Publication Data

    O Canainn, Tomás
        Seán Ó Riada: his life and work
        1. Ó Riada, Seán, 1931-1971 2. Musicians – Ireland –
        Biography
        I. Title
        780.9'2

        ISBN 1903464404

Typesetting by The Collins Press

This book is printed on uncoated paper manufactured with the greatest
possible care for the environment.

Printed in Ireland by Betaprint

Cover photograph of Seán Ó Riada: Ayoub

CONTENTS

ACKNOWLEDGEMENTS

The author is happy to acknowledge the assistance he received from the following during the preparation of this book:

Louise Verling, Peadar Ó Riada, Rachel Ní Riada, Walter Verling, Seán Ó Sé, Ronnie McShane, Seán Lucy, Gerard Victory, John Montague, Dónal Casey, Éamonn de Buitléar, Lally Lamb de Buitléar, Fr. J.J. Greehy, Dónal Ó Liatháin, Riobárd Mac Górain, Seán Mac Réamoinn, Venetia O'Sullivan, Treasa O'Driscoll, Fachtna Ó hAnnracháin, Paddy Murphy, Helen Ó Canainn, Liz Cranitch, Seán Mac Mathúna, Áine Uí Chanainn, An tAthair Pádraig Breathnach, Dónal Ó Mathúna, Aloys Fleischmann, Roy Hammond, Fr White, Billy Browne, John Cagney, An tAthair M. Ó Crualaoi, Joe Terry, Noel Campbell, Seán Ó Tuama, John A. Murphy, Seán Ó Coileáin, Gloria McGowran, Garech de Brún, Edward Delaney, Marie Whelan-Powell, Pat Lucy, Seán Ó Baoill, Louis Marcus, Seán Ó Mórdha, An tAthair Donncha Ó Conchúir, Larry Egar, Brian Lynch, Ian Lee, Gareth Costelloe, Thomas Kinsella, Tony Canniffe, Kathleen Barrington, Bridget Doolan, Colm O'Sullivan, Dave Owens, Claire Goggin, An Br. Ó Ceallaigh, Br Paul Donovan, Seán Ó Cíomháin, Séamus Ó Cíomháin, Tomás Mistéil, Michael Bradley, Bene McAteer, Brian Jack, Paddy Ring, Nicholas Carolan, University College Cork, RTÉ, Gael Linn, Claddagh Records, Farranferris College, The Abbey Theatre, *The Irish Times, Irish Examiner* for photographs.

INTRODUCTION

Ireland of the 1950s, isolated from Europe and still recovering from the effects of the Second World War, lacked much in self-esteem. But those same 1950s were Seán Ó Riada's twenties – when his burgeoning talent had all the energy of a fiercely burning star. That star was first manifest to the general public when he composed the film score for the film *Mise Eire*, which became hugely popular. It was followed by other film scores, large orchestral works, songs, masses and the formation of his own traditional group – the model for the plethora of modern groups that travel the world and who may not even be aware of their real origin. Seán's intense life and talent were destined to burn themselves out far too soon. He died at forty.

I have interviewed scores of his friends, acquaintances and members of his family to piece together this story of his life, for Seán showed different sides of his multi-facetted personality to different people. No single person knew the complete Seán Ó Riada.

I knew him as a friend with whom I could play a few tunes and as a colleague in University College Cork, throughout the last seven years of his life. For the last three of those years I was a student of his in the Music Department and took over his Irish music lectures for some years after his death. However, it is only now that I feel I have glimpsed the complete Ó Riada, for Seán was much more than a great musician.

My story is what we call in Irish *cloch ar a charn* – another small stone on the monument to his memory, his music and to the work of art that his life was.

CHAPTER 1

E A R L Y   L I F E   I N   A D A R E

Seán Ó Riada was born under his English name of John Reidy in Cork on 1 August 1931, notwithstanding the fact that the family lived in Adare, County Limerick at the time. His mother had had a series of unsuccessful pregnancies before this, so it was decided that she should go to the Erinville Hospital in Cork for the birth. The new baby, the first child of Julia Creedon and Seán Reidy, was their only offspring until 1935, when his sister Louise was born in the Croom Union. In later years, when Julia felt her daughter might be getting a little above herself, she would remind her jokingly that it was in the Union she first saw the light of day. The fact was that Julia was in charge of the maternity unit in the hospital at the time.

Both of young Seán's parents were of farming stock. His father hailed from Kilmichil in west Clare and was a member of the Garda Síochána, stationed in Adare in the early days. His great-grandfather was a stone-mason and there was at least one local headstone of his with a Latin inscription. He signed his work S. Ó Riada – a name that his great-grandson would not adopt for many years yet. The Reidys were a musical family and Seán knew that his grandmother, on his father's side, could play the concertina. He never knew her, as she died young. His father could play the violin and often had a tune with the well-known Clare fiddler, Patrick Kelly.

Ó Riada's mother was from Droim Riabhach in west Cork. She was the youngest of eight children and her mother died giving birth. Julia, whose mother could play both piano and harmonium, was musically talented, with a good ear, and could play a tune on nearly any instrument. In her youth she had taken violin lessons from a travelling fiddle teacher who visited a house in the district regularly.

Seán's son Peadar tells a story of the time Julia tried to play a tune on his Clarke's tin whistle and didn't do very well. Unknown to Peadar, she spent the next few weeks practising and then one evening she asked him to sit down, so that she could play a few hornpipes for him on the whistle. To his surprise, she played them very well indeed, but then put down the whistle and never played it again. She had done what she wanted to do – to show him that if he could play the instrument, she could do the same.

Julia always regretted she never had professional training in music and, on discovering that her son had music in him, she decided to have him properly trained. She had missed an opportunity in her youth to go to university, when she was a nurse. The chief surgeon in the hospital was keen that she should attend University College Cork to train in medicine, but her own father would not hear of it. As it happened subsequently, Seán's father was just as conservative when Louise wanted to go to University, but Julia saw to it that the younger generation would not lose their opportunity.

So it transpired that young Seán would cycle the nine miles from Adare to Limerick every Saturday to take piano, organ and violin lessons. His violin teacher was Granville Metcalfe and Van de Velde his organ teacher. Louise could not remember, when I interviewed her, who taught her brother piano. By the time Louise began violin lessons, Julia had arranged that Metcalfe would come regularly to their house in Adare, where he would teach other local students as well.

Julia believed that one should read printed music as one would read any other book: on every visit to Limerick she would bring back a bundle of music for her children – which explains why Seán and Louise were always excellent sight-readers. For them, playing or singing new music was a mixture of fun and pleasure – never a chore.

As a six-week old baby, Seán became very ill, almost to the point of death. His mother, thereafter, was very solicitous for his health and worried about him continuously if she did not know where he was. On her son's journeys into Limerick for lessons, she would allow a certain time for cycling, an hour, perhaps, for his music lessons, half an hour for his reading in the locals bookshop (where he perfected his speed-reading techniques!) and half an hour for his cycle ride back to Adare. If Seán was more than five or ten minutes late, she would be out on the road, anxiously awaiting his return.

Seán's son Peadar remembers lodging with his granny, in her house off College Road, when he was a student at UCC. Julia would allow him eight minutes to get from the Music Department to her home after his lectures. She and her husband would be waiting for him, if he were more than a few minutes late. She took her responsibilities to her grandson just as seriously as she had done for her own children.

Seán and Louise had a strict upbringing, for Julia was a strong character who would not put up with a task badly done. Her word was law and she had to be obeyed. They dropped everything when their mother called and Julia accepted no excuses. She was extremely proud of her son and was not shy about telling him that he was talented. The young Seán attended the Christian Brothers' primary school in Adare and some of Julia's former neighbours remember her boasting that he was the cleverest lad in Munster! Who would gainsay that now?

There was always a certain strain in family matters which was due to fear – the mother's fear for her child. Seán had appendicitis at the age of nine, which was not properly attended to and which turned to peritonitis. He was very near death again and was only saved by a four-hour operation. Julia's protective instincts were reinforced by this new danger to her son.

Julia's husband, Seán Reidy, was a quiet, welcoming man. His chief joys were to fish in the river, for he was an excellent fisherman, or sit by his own fireside, reading a book or playing the fiddle. He never raised a hand to his son and valued peace highly, especially at home. Daily mass and communion were the norm.

He was a sergeant in the gardaí, but was not interested in further promotion. A sergeant's pay in those days was not great and the family were not well-off. It was often suggested to him that he should apply for promotion, the implication being that he would get it, for he was good at his job, but he did not want the additional unnecessary stress that it would bring. He had his own way of maintaining the rule of law in Adare: he didn't go looking for late drinkers in the pub but usually appeared on the street, talking to his friends, just after closing time. That was the signal to the pub owners that it was time to shut up shop. There was a story that one of them tended to delay closing until he'd heard a knock on the back door in a certain rhythm. That was the final warning!

Seán Reidy was a brave man. He had been a republican in Clare in his youth but that was never mentioned after he joined the Gardaí. He was badly wounded on one occasion when, totally unarmed, he tried to persuade an armed youth who was involved in a robbery to submit and hand over his gun. The gun was fired and the brave sergeant was lucky to escape with his life.

But Seán Ó Riada regarded his father as weak and his mother Julia as the strong partner, though that was too simplistic a view of the situation. However, it is not inconceivable that this was the reason why Seán, in later life, became quite a stern father to his own children.

CHAPTER 2

T O   S C H O O L   I N   C O R K

Seán left primary school in Adare in 1943 and enrolled in St Finbarr's College, Farranferris, Cork, in September of that year. On the same day, another young lad entered the college and they were put into the same class, Junior Three, the class for the best students. They had just two years of study before sitting for their first public examination, the Intermediate Certificate of the Department of Education.

The classmate was John Joe Greehy, who was to become a very well-known scripture scholar in later years. Like Seán, he was the son of a sergeant in the Gardaí and they lived in Kilmallock in County Cork. They had something else in common, as both mothers wanted their sons to continue their piano studies in Farranferris. John Joe had already taken some examinations of the Royal Irish Academy of Music.

Their piano teacher was Aloys Fleischmann, whose son Aloys, destined to become Professor of Music in UCC in later years, had already gone through Farranferris as a student. Fleischmann senior was an excellent teacher who had come from Germany to take up the post of organist in St Mary's Cathedral. In his early years at Farranferris, Seán practised piano assiduously under the direction of Herr Fleischmann and attended Willie Brady's violin lessons in Cork. He also took organ lessons in the cathedral from his piano teacher.

Some of Seán's classmates remember him as a sensitive, musical person, with creative tendencies. Most of them saw him as being different from themselves – an outsider. He was intellectual – they knew that - and scholarship was important in Farranferris in those days. But sport was very highly regarded, particularly hurling, and Seán did not shine in that department. Among the students the game was of paramount importance and a lack of ability on the hurling field was more significant than any amount of brains.

Seán played in one internal match and did not impress. In fact, in his frustration, he lost his temper and struck an opponent a considerable blow with the camán. His failure at hurling further isolated him from his fellow students.

Farranferris was a boarding seminary for the diocese, though that did not mean that all of its students were destined for the priesthood. A large percentage did, however, proceed to Maynooth or one of the other clerical colleges, as those who wished to join the priesthood in the diocese of Cork and Ross were obliged to attend Farranferris for a minimum number of years.

There was a high standard of Greek and Latin taught in those days, as Maynooth set high store by the classics. The teachers of those subjects in Farranferris were Doctor (later Canon) Connolly and Father Michael Roche. Their best students attained a high standard – none better than Seán and his friend J.J. Greehy.

Greehy remembers that the College had not won a hurling cup for some time and that it was Seán Ó Riada who gained their only trophy, by getting first prize at Feis Maitiú in the Shanahan competition for violin. He won a number of competitions in those years. Evidently the President of the College, Canon T.F. Duggan, complained to Seán about a report in the papers after he had won the Shanahan Cup. 'Why didn't you say you were attending Farranferris College, instead of saying you were from Adare?' asked the Canon. Seán did not answer him, but merely shrugged his shoulders. Some of Seán's classmates remember Father Roche teasing the hurling boys in the class. 'You all march out,' said he, 'with drums beating and flags flying – and then back you come with empty hands, trailing your flags after you. But look at Reidy there, who slipped out the gate with his violin tucked humbly under his arm – and wasn't he the one to bring back the cup!'

One of the teachers who understood Seán's talent was the priest An t-Athair Tadhg Ó Murchú. He used to hold special evenings in the College on Sundays, when he would teach songs in Irish and have students perform. Ó Riada, playing violin, instead of piano, was the normal accompanist on these occasions. A student of those days, now Father Ó Crualaoi, remembers assisting on accordion. Ó Riada also often played the organ at mass in Farranferris.

The students were sometimes permitted to go to concerts in Cork – not a common procedure in city schools at the time. They were allowed out to recitals of the Cork Symphony Orchestra, which was, of course, conducted by Aloys Fleischmann, who, as well as being an old boy of the College, was also the son of their music teacher.

Canon Connolly, who presented regular Sunday night concerts in the Palace Theatre in MacCurtáin Street, asked Ó Riada to play there. This was a big occasion for the lad, as the usual artists were well-known names in the city. There was a big audience of Cork people and students in attendance. Some of Seán's classmates remember that he was playing classical music on the violin until he realised that his listeners were not really paying much attention, so he changed to céilí music and got huge applause. After that night Seán's stock soared in Farranferris and even though he was still a loner, his talent was recognised by all.

After completing the Inter Certificate examination, Seán decided to go on to his senior studies, rather than repeating a year and doing the examination again, something common at the time, as his mother wished him to prepare for the Leaving Certificate Examination. Students repeated the Inter Cert in the hope of getting a public scholarship, which would increase the college's reputation as an educational establishment. Even though J.J. Greehy remained in fourth year to repeat the examination, he was given the privileges of a senior student. One of those privileges was being in an upstairs room, far away from the packed dormitories. The two friends shared a room from then on.

J.J. Greehy remembers that Seán used to discuss everything with him – not only the events of the day in the outside world but all about the books he was reading – and he was an avid reader. He would often suggest that Greehy should put an unusual twist into an essay for the English teacher, or perhaps slip in something funny or sarcastic, for a laugh. Even then, Greehy remembers thinking there was a bright future in literature or a connected discipline for Ó Riada, who had a phenomenal memory and intellect, and whose general conversation was so far above his fellow students that they failed to make sense of it.

Even in those days, Seán had begun to question authority, whether it came from the Church, the State, or the school. He had little regard for the conservative spiritualism that surrounded him and constantly questioned why he should have to confess regularly. Matters like these were under frequent discussion by the two friends in the upper room and J.J. Greehy (who was later to be President of Clonliffe College) freely acknowledges that Ó Riada had a considerable influence on him in matters of religion and nationalism.

Notwithstanding Seán's complaints about religion, either he himself – or more likely his mother, on his behalf – harboured thoughts of the priesthood, as he left Farranferris in 1947 to go for a year to St Munchin's College in Limerick. This was a necessary step for aspiring priests of the Limerick diocese, which was the diocese in which the family resided.

His Farranferris classmates of those days do not remember Seán having any special interest in the Irish language, though every student in the College spoke Irish well, due to the teaching of An t-Athair Tadhg Ó Murchú. Many spent part of their summer holidays in the Kerry Gaeltacht, in a small house, known as the *bothán*, organised by the same priest. Strangely enough, Ó Riada never did.

It was An t-Athair Tadhg, many years later, who invited Seán to spend a period in his new hostel, which replaced the original *bothán* – *Brú na Gráige*. Seán's visit to west Kerry was destined to effect a major change in Ó Riada's subsequent life.

CHAPTER 3

C L A S S I C I S T   O R   M U S I C I A N ?

Whensed once by a foreign musician what he had studied at
University, Seán's reply to his interviewer was 'Classics!' It was
only partly true.

He entered University College Cork in 1948 and began his First
Arts course with Irish, Greek, Latin, English and Music as his subjects.
He passed his First Arts examination, attaining First Honours in Music.

In the academic year 1949-50 he took Greek and Latin in Second
Arts and registered for First Music in the B. Mus. course, having been
granted permission by the President to so do. He failed Greek and Latin
in the summer examinations and did not take up his available option of
repeating them in the autumn. He did, however, get Second honours in
First Music. He was unable to continue with the BA course, but took
Second Music that year and eventually completed his B. Mus. with
Second Honours in 1952.

Professor Fleischmann often told me that it was not as a result of
study that Seán achieved his B. Mus., as he rarely did the musical exer-
cises set out by the professor. Not only that, but he often did not show
up for his lectures. It would not have been so noticeable in other circumstances, but he was Fleischmann's only B. Mus. student, and the

poor professor, living in Passage West at the time, used to cycle to Cork to give his lecture, only to discover he had no student! Not unnaturally, this led to more than one serious confrontation and the professor remembers his student crying when he realised the enormity of what he had done. Fleischmann always said that Seán got the B. Mus. through sheer talent, but he maintained that Seán was the cleverest and most musical student he ever had.

Seán Lucy, who was later to become Professor of English in UCC, first encountered Seán in the autumn term in 1950. Both were seasoned students by this time, but had not previously met, though they had been in the same Latin class in the previous year.

There was a group of friends in UCC at the time – male and female students, who met regularly to discuss affairs and drink coffee in the college restaurant, known as 'The Rest'. Ó Riada was to become a member of the group later and even though the marriages of Lucy and Ó Riada resulted from acquaintances made in those days, there was no obvious romance in the group: they were much more interested in the Dramatic Society, in films or in trips to the countryside. The original members included Pat Kennedy, who was later to marry Seán Lucy, Helen Maloney, a medical student, Dónal Murphy, who was studying engineering and Seán Lucy. Pat knew Marie Whelan, who was to marry the High Sheriff of Cork, Collins-Powell. A friend of Marie's, Ruth Coughlan, became a member of the group and was eventually to marry Seán Ó Riada.

In autumn 1950 a new member, unlike the others, joined the group. He was Ultan McEligott, who had come from Canada to study philosophy under Professor James O'Mahony. McEligott was older and more mature than the others, with habits they found a little strange. He was fashionably dressed and had an apartment of his own: he did his own cooking, whereas the other students were all lodgers in digs. He had wine on the table at mealtimes, was a good talker with a fine sense of humour and, all in all, added much status and sophistication to the group.

Ultan and Seán Lucy were in the Savoy restaurant one day, when an argument arose between Ó Riada, who had come to their table, and Lucy. It resulted from a discussion on religion and the existence or non-existence of a next life. McEligott and Lucy were surprised to find that young Ó Riada was not what they would regard as a normal Catholic, but a follower of Sartre and a believer in black French existensialism. He didn't seem to go along with normal metaphysics, but claimed that the absurd was at the heart of everything.

Eventually Lucy and McEligott rose to leave, as they wanted to be rid of this talkative student. They were surprised to find that he was following them, hoping, perhaps, for further argument or at least a continuation of the discussion. Lucy remembers being very dissatisfied on that occasion, either with Ó Riada and his opinions, or even with his own part in their argument.

Some days later, he accosted Lucy in the quadrangle and, half shyly and half aggressively, asked him if he would listen to some music of his. They went to a music room over the President's office and Ó Riada sat down at the piano and began to play. Lucy remembered the music as being vaguely like that of Debussy, with long silvery runs that would remind you of a summer morning on a stony beach – all clean and bright. Lucy reckoned their friendship began when he told Ó Riada that he liked it very much.

Seán Lucy was a well-known figure among the students in those days, as he had already published poetry and short stories. Ó Riada was satisfied that someone like him thought his music good and, more importantly, thought the young composer had talent. Lucy remembered being convinced that Ó Riada had in his heart and soul the real thing – genius.

Ó Riada joined the group after this and soon he and Ruth Coughlan became an 'item'. Various students of the time to whom I have spoken remember Ó Riada as a bit of a loner, who did not talk much about himself or his background, but who was important in the social life of the college, as he played piano regularly at dances in the Rest and in a number of dance-halls in the city. Ruth Coughlan and Pat Kennedy were regular patrons of these functions.

From 1949-52 Ó Riada inhabited two very distinct worlds – the academic life of the University, and the world of pop, jazz and dance music, which he practised assiduously outside his B. Mus. course.

Billy Browne, whose band played regularly for dances in the Arcadia ballroom in Cork, was looking for a pianist and Ó Riada was recommended to him for his group, Billy Browne and his Music. The bass player in the band, John Cagney, told me that he was the person who recommended the student, who was then invited to their regular Monday night practice. It did not matter what music was put in front of him, he was able to perform it expertly. Billy remembers that he was particularly keen on jazz and, as far as Browne knew, had no interest in Irish music.

Ó Riada spent a few years playing with the band in Cork, Kerry, Tipperary and Waterford. They played mostly for dances in those days, with, perhaps, a few Sunday evening concerts in either the Palace or the Capitol. They would normally play for two or three dances a week.

Billy told me that in later years, though Seán was working in Dublin, he used to come into Billy's shop in Academy Street, Cork, sometimes to buy seed for his garden. On one such occasion they had a long chat about old times and when Seán went out, a girl who was working for Billy said to him: 'I didn't know that you were a friend of Seán Ó Riada.' 'I'm not,' said Billy, 'I never met him.' 'What do you mean?' she replied. 'Weren't you talking to him there now and hasn't he just gone out of the shop?' 'Of course not,' said Billy: 'That's John Reidy who used to play with us in the band years ago.' 'Well,' she said, 'look at the telly tonight at eight o'clock and you'll see I'm right.' That was how Billy Browne discovered that his John Reidy was the famous Seán Ó Riada.

Billy remembered the first arrangement of dance music that Seán provided for the band. It was *Summertime*, he thought, but it was far too complicated for the average dance band, though it would have been a very good concert piece. As a piece for dancing, however, it was a failure.

Billy praised Ó Riada highly as a pianist who could do an excellent solo spot in the interval of a dance or as a jazz pianist with drum accompaniment. He had no doubt Seán could earn a living at that kind of music and he remembers him as a shy person. He was always at his ease in chatting to the other musicians and enjoyed the banter when they were going to or coming from gigs by car. He kept himself apart and drank little.

Billy admitted they were not aware that they had a genius in their midst. 'We were all young then and we weren't looking for a genius – all we wanted was a pianist who could play the notes the way we wanted them and he could certainly do that!'

Billy advised me to go and talk to John Cagney – the man who had first recommended Ó Riada to him. It seems that Cagney and other musicians had a weekly jazz session in Gregg Hall on the South Mall. One night John noticed a thin young fellow sitting alone – watching and listening. John spoke to him after the session and when he heard that he was a music student who could play piano, he invited him to his home, which was just across the road. John asked him to play something and was amazed at the excellence of his playing. 'Thank God he was not playing over there tonight,' he said to himself.

Cagney had a small group who played for parties, weddings, army dances, etc., Among the group were Dónal Casey from Cobh, Pat Mitchell on drums and John Cagney on bass. Ó Riada sometimes sat in with them on piano and they were all impressed with his arrangements. Cagney told me that the young student could arrange music for any kind of musical group, though he admitted his music could be difficult and complicated. 'His talent started where the rest of ours finished.' Cagney had a story about the time Seán was accompanist to an English tenor who was to sing in the Savoy in 1950 or 1951. The poor man had a cold and was very worried about the high C he had to sing in one of the arias. He confided his fears to Seán as they were about to start the concert. 'Don't worry your head about it,' said Seán. 'I'll transpose it down to B and you'll be alright.' He did and everything was great. The tenor kept telling people that nobody else could have done it on first sight, as Seán had.

There were a few sessions in Cagney's house at which Bobby Lamb, recognised as one of the world's best trombonists, was present. Lamb and Ó Riada were playing together for the first time and Cagney remembers Ó Riada, before he started, joining his hands so that the fingers interlaced and then bending them to make his fingers crack loudly. 'Well Bobby,' he said, 'what will we play – jazz, pop or classical?'

Cagney felt very strongly that Lamb's skill had a considerable influence on Ó Riada and, equally, Lamb learned much from Seán, who spent some six months lodging in Cagney's house in his first year at UCC. Cagney's mother listened to them often and tried to induce them to do something with Irish music in modern attire. Though they did not do this at the time, the family liked to think that Mrs Cagney may have had some influence on both Lamb, who composed *Clann Lir* later and maybe even on the composer of *Mise Eire*.

John Cagney told me that he felt Ó Riada was more of a working musician than an academic and he had no doubt that Seán should have continued as a top composer, rather than returning to the University as an academic in the 1960s as he lacked inspiration in that situation.

Seán Ó Sé told me about a drummer, Joe Terry, who hailed from Albert Road in Cork and played with Ó Riada in Parknasilla Hotel in the summer of 1951. Their small group comprised Bill Brierley, piano, Denis Cronin, saxophone and clarinet, Joe Terry on drums and Ó Riada on violin. Full board was provided for the musicians, with first-class meals and every day free until night time, except for an hour between four and five, when afternoon tea or coffee was served for the guests, to music from the quartet – a soothing mixture of pop and light classics.

Joe played every summer at Parknasilla but Ó Riada spent only one season there. The two of them shared a room and Joe remembers Seán doing a lot of study.

They would play for dancing in the hotel from 9pm until midnight. The music was not arranged specially for the group, but Brierley played from a piano version and the other three would busk along as best they could. Joe remembers that Ó Riada had occasional solos in the afternoon session, but in the evening it was all in together, playing gently, since that was what the hotel owners wanted.

Ó Riada did not play piano with the group, as Brierley was the official pianist. He was very particular about his status in that regard and would not consider allowing anyone else usurp him. However, on wet days Seán had a habit of staying indoors and playing the piano for his own enjoyment. Gradually, it became known that there was a real master at the piano and people began to come in regularly to listen. But after a few wet days, the piano was locked to prevent the emergence of a second pianist. It was only opened subsequently for the evening sessions.

Seán played for some time with a short-lived group known as The Kamble Kombo, directed by Noel Campbell. They first came together as a trio – Barney Mulgrew on saxophone and clarinet, Ó Riada on piano and Noel himself on guitar. Noel told me they gave the group that title because it was short, snappy and small enough to fit on their music stands, as they were all readers of music. Noel knew that Seán was an excellent pianist and a good reader, which was why he invited him to play with them. He also hoped that Ó Riada might do some arrangements for the group – which he did. Noel showed me an arrangement of *Small Hotel* which Seán had done. It was one of a number that included the Irish national anthem which, in those days, was always played after the last dance of the evening.

Their first gig was at Christmas in the Grand Hotel in Crosshaven, organised by Kevin O'Shea. Noel remembers Seán smoking Sobrani cigars with a gold seal. In keeping with his French style, he would wear a dark beret on such occasions. Ó Riada did not think much of standard band arrangements: he preferred South American music like samba, rumba and cha-cha. The band sometimes played such music, with Seán leading on piano and the rest following.

Back at UCC some students of the time remember Seán as unkempt, grubby and unhealthy looking; white-faced, tall and thin, dressed in black and seeming to model himself on the Joycean French style. As far as he was concerned, *The Portrait of the Artist as a Young Man* and *Ulysses* were holy books. Seán Lucy remembers him as volatile, introspective and unpredictable. His mood could change in a moment from happy and carefree to one that was bitter and even hostile. In argument he always preferred to win than to find a real answer and his somewhat superior and overbearing approach often made him enemies.

In aesthetic matters, however, Lucy felt that Ó Riada was nearer to McElligot and himself artistically than he was in matters of religion. Both were interested in modern poetry, especially that of Ezra Pound, and in other modern developments in the arts in general. Above all his other interests, Ó Riada seemed to be on a higher plane when he played piano – as if he had gone into another world, where no one could get to him.

During spring 1951 Seán Lucy and Pat Kennedy fell in love and were more or less inseparable, until Pat finished her BA and left UCC in the autumn. In that period Lucy and Ó Riada did not have much contact but this changed in the academic year 1951-52, when both were in their final year. Ruth Coughlan and Ó Riada were together much of that year and the three friends often had meals together in Ruth's father's home. In this period, Lucy was helping Ruth with her English course. The three enjoyed wonderful times of music and chat.

Sean Ó Riada at his 1952 B. Mus. Graduation.

It was a friendship that was to continue long after they left UCC – right up to the tragic deaths of both Ruth and Ó Riada.

Lucy remembered the great love Ruth and Seán had for one another – two headstrong young people, certain of themselves and accustomed to getting their own way. Even though they differed in many respects, their differences somehow integrated into a fulfilment of their partnership. Their love was very important in Ó Riada's life – something stable and unchanging, even when outside influences threatened it.

With the departure of Pat Kennedy to work in London and Helen Maloney to study in Dublin, the group ceased to exist, though Lucy and Ó Riada still met once a week for lunch. At one of these meetings Ó Riada suggested that he should teach his friend to speak Irish. Lucy had been reared in the country and educated at home by his mother, before being sent to Glenstal to finish his education. It was decided there that, since young Lucy was good at German, he should continue his study of that language in Glenstal, rather than try to compete with the other boys at Irish – a language they had all been studying for some ten years previously.

Lucy had read much in Irish literature before this time, but all in the English language, so Ó Riada decided that his friend should learn Irish from him. But Seán's language teaching did not last long, after Ó Riada spent at least half an hour insisting on the correct pronunciation of the slender 't', as opposed to the broad 't' in the word *toitín*. Lucy soon realised that he was not going to make much progress in the language if Ó Riada continued to be fussy about minute details, so he asked him to teach him a song in Irish, which Seán did. It was *Droimín Donn Dílis*. Lucy insisted that Ó Riada knew Irish well at the time, long before his 'road to Damascus' conversion in the Kerry Gaeltacht in the late 1950s.

Ó Riada had a very strange sense of humour: Lucy remembered it as concentrating on wild exaggeration – the sort of thing that one might find in old Irish tales. He liked telling bawdy yarns of the type that mixed sex and fantasy in equal measure. Lucy felt that it was the sexual energy in such stories that made them attractive to Ó Riada.

By the end of 1952, Ó Riada's style of dress was changing for the better. Some attributed it to Ruth's influence, but whether she actively suggested changes or whether Seán made them because she would be pleased, is open to question. He still wore black, of course, with a high-necked sweater – no collar and tie yet, very different to the other students who were conservative dressers.

By December 1952, Ruth moved to Dublin and Ó Riada was hell-bent on finding cash, so that they could soon marry. He got an interesting financial offer from a legal friend of his, Kevin O'Shea. The Grand Hotel in Crosshaven was bankrupt and Kevin had been appointed receiver and administrator of its affairs, with a view to selling it. He offered Seán £3 a week and free lodging to look after the hotel. Ó Riada badly needed the money and wanted to take the job, but he was terrified of loneliness. Given his superstitions and his belief in the supernatural, he could not live alone in a huge empty hotel by the seaside in midwinter.

Ó Riada had a chat with Lucy about the project. 'Look,' he said, 'this is how it is: you're a big strapping fellow with a rifle and you know how to use it. As well as that, you have a large knife. What do you say to being my bodyguard in this big hotel, to protect me from things natural and supernatural?' Lucy was interested, since he had begun researching T.S. Eliot for his Masters thesis and needed to do a lot of reading that winter. He agreed, on condition that they split the money between them, but Ó Riada protested that he needed the cash urgently. They settled eventually on £1 a week and free board.

The two friends went down to Crosshaven by bus, loaded down with clothes, books and all their paraphernalia, not to mention the rifle and the knife! They stayed for a few months, until spring 1953 and in that period they got to know each other particularly well. They shared one bedroom on the first floor, with a view over the river, but spent most of their time in the kitchen, either cooking or talking – usually both. At other times, they would go into a large room with a piano, where Seán would play all kinds of music. They jointly composed a bawdy song in French, which began: *Monsieur la sentinelle, attendez au pissoir.* They often sang it together, late at night, along the streets of Crosshaven, on their way back from dinner at Kevin O'Shea's house.

More than anything else, they spent long hours discussing life and Ó Riada's fear of death and even of sleep – as he did not want to lose control of his intellect or consciousness, even for a short time. He feared death – not for the pain that it might bring, but for the loss of self and self-awareness, which he saw as its inevitable partners. Ó Riada's personality was a curious mixture of scepticism, which made him doubt anything he heard, and a simple but firm belief in matters supernatural. He often told the story of the barefoot woman coming towards him one evening and of his certain knowledge that she was someone from the other world. He tried to pray and could not, but kept his eyes away from her as she passed. He knew all the time, though, that he'd have to turn eventually and look after her, though he was certain there would be no one there when he looked – and there wasn't! He believed in ghosts and devils, though he was also, at the time, an agnostic of sorts.

Ó Riada's fears came from within. Lucy remembers coming back to the hotel once and finding Ó Riada in his room, white as a sheet and petrified with fear. 'Thank God you're back,' Ó Riada said. 'There was something from the other world about to show itself to me.' Lucy himself often felt more at ease when Ó Riada had gone to Cork for the day, as the fear of evil spirits was becoming infectious.

Lucy's opinion of Ó Riada was interesting: 'He was an intellectual with an unusual imagination. I have never known anyone with such a quick and mature intellect. I couldn't really say he was logical and he certainly wasn't a philosopher in the narrowest sense of the word, but he could use logic and philosophy, either to win an argument or to further his own creative work. He wasn't always a seeker of abstract truth, but rather sought a personal truth that suited the particular project he happened to be working on at the time. He was fiercely competitive in argument and would make his point energetically, so that one had to struggle to put an opposing view. Aggression and threat were always a part of his style – and many were put off by it. Seán was never above employing a specious argument, if that suited his cause. Notwithstanding all that, we enjoyed our interminable discussions –

day and night!'

Lucy acknowledged that it was Ó Riada who guided him towards Joyce and Flann O'Brien. They would read these authors often to each other during this period in Crosshaven, as well as translations of the Theban plays of Sophocles from a Penguin book Lucy had bought.

After Easter 1952 Lucy went to London to do research and be with Pat Kennedy. Ó Riada was not satisfied with this development, saying it was not right that Lucy should leave him alone, as he badly needed the money he got for looking after the hotel and could not do it by himself. Lucy asked his father, Colonel Lucy, to go down to Ó Riada from Rowanscourt, where he lived. The two got on very well and Lucy reckoned his father, who had at one time worked for Radio Éireann, gave Ó Riada a very good reference when Seán later applied for the post of Assistant Director of Music in that organisation.

Seán Lucy remembered being back in Cork around the time Ó Riada was to go for interview. His former, rather scruffy room-mate was transformed. He now wore a new grey suit of top quality, complete with shirt and tie, brightly polished shoes and a smart felt halt to complete the ensemble. One thing was clear: a chapter of Ó Riada's life was closing and another opening up before him.

The most important element in that new life was Seán's marriage to Ruth on 1 September 1953 in the Honan Chapel, University College Cork. The second important element was the possibility of a new job in Dublin with Radio Éireann.

CHAPTER 4

R A D I O   É I R E A N N

When the vacancy for Assistant Director of Music in Radio Éireann was advertised in 1953, informed opinion within the organisation was that Kevin Roche, the internal candidate, who was already in the Music Department, would be successful. However, the Director, Fachtna Ó h-Annracháin, told Kevin Roche, some time after he had done the interview, that he would not get the job as a dark horse from Cork by the name of Reidy had done an outstanding interview and would be the new Assistant Director. It transpired later that the young Cork applicant had spent a considerable time during the interview arguing with one of his interviewers about philosophy. After a three-month trial period he was given the job.

For the next couple of years, Kevin, Venetia O'Sullivan and Ó Riada worked together in room 339 in Henry Street, with Kevin responsible for the Symphony Orchestra, Venetia writing scripts about music and Seán assisting the Director in organising music generally. There was a good atmosphere in the room between the Dubliners and the pale-faced young Corkman. They liked his sense of humour and were impressed by his broad musical knowledge.

One day, when Venetia was absent, a script was required urgently for an orchestral concert, where Mozart's *Jupiter* symphony was to be played. Seán wrote an outstanding script – almost a thesis – based on the theory that Mozart's last three symphonies were written as a unit, and he defended his position logically. Ó Riada was himself very proud of this gem, which he completed before lunchtime.

In an interview I did with the late Gerard Victory, he remembered Ó Riada's arrival at Radio Éireann. Gerard was not connected with the Music Department at the time, even though he was composing a lot of music himself. It is interesting that he was to become Director of Music in the station, years later. A friendship grew between him and the young Corkman. Victory remembers Ó Riada conversing on a range of topics – from Stravinsky to French and ancient Greek literature, not to mention bawdy topics and the bad effect of censorship on life in Ireland.

Gerard remembers Seán in those days as being informally dressed, describing him as a 'Gaeltacht man'. Ó Riada would not have seen himself in this light: he always presented himself as a musician and composer who wanted to make a big name for himself. In many ways Seán was a loner in Radio Éireann. There was still a Civil Service atmosphere in the radio station at the time, with formally dressed employees, including Gerard Victory, close together in cramped offices with little technical equipment. Television and Donnybrook were still years away! Most of them recognised that an exotic bird had landed among them when Seán arrived from Cork.

After Ó Riada discovered that Victory was interested in serious music, they had many conversations on Stravinsky, Schoenberg, Webern and Berg.

Ó Riada was a talkative person – all who knew him in those days concur on that. He felt a continual compulsion to give information to others, especially on literature: Victory remembered him talking often about a little-known nineteenth-century author, Pierre Lowÿs whose novels were based on life in ancient Greece and Egypt. There was plenty in his writings to scandalise Irish people of the 1950s, but they did not get to read them, due to censorship, which Seán spent much time denouncing, as he did other aspects of Irish cultural and political life.

In his early days in Radio Éireann, Seán was given to 'putting on airs' and was not slow to express his opinions when talking about music or the arts in Ireland. Some of the staff liked him for that and some did not. One of his best friends in the organisation was Doctor Arthur Duff, Assistant Director of Music. He was a Protestant, who had been a Director of Music in the Army. Duff did not speak Irish, which was why he had been passed over for the job of Director of Music in Radio Éireann when that post had become available. He was, therefore, a disappointed man, who felt he had not got the promotion he deserved. One would not have expected such different characters to become friends, but they did, due to their intense mutual interest in classical music.

In early 1950, Ireland was not a part of the new movement that was overtaking and transforming European music – atonality. Old traditions were being transformed, as atonality was banishing the concept that all music was based on a tonal centre, implying that certain notes of the scale had more importance than others. Schoenberg was the originator of atonality in the 1920s and he was followed by Webern and Berg. Their music began to be seriously discussed by professional musicians on the continent after the Second World War, but even in the 1950s, professional musicians in Ireland were scarcely aware of it, while the general concert-going public would not have known of it at all. Yet this was the gospel Ó Riada was preaching to Duff, who, initially at least, had no great sympathy with it.

Radio Éireann in the 1950s had a fairly conservative policy in regard to what music they would accept from composers. Arrangements of Irish music were generally acceptable but not newly composed music, especially not from their own staff. It was Arthur Duff who was responsible for what was accepted and, more importantly, what was not – and Ó Riada's cause was probably not harmed by his friendship with Duff. It seems that few pieces submitted by Seán were refused, particularly subsequent to the acceptance of his *Hercules Dux Ferrariae* in 1957. This work had been shown to the Italian conductor Carlo Franci before being accepted by Radio Éireann and he had praised it highly. It was Franci, years later, who conducted the London Symphony Orchestra when the work was being recorded for Claddagh Records.

Seán found much of his work as Assistant Director inspiring: he enjoyed arranging concerts and details of orchestral performances but there were other aspects of the job which he disliked intensely. In those days Radio Éireann would receive hundreds of letters weekly – many of them complaints, others from TDs, musicians or their agents, asking that certain bands be given an airing on radio. It gradually became apparent that Seán was not the most suitable person for this kind of office work. He would set about it diligently but might then drift towards another aspect of the job. At other times he would be attracted by something new and exciting, until he tired of that as well. The result was that mundane office tasks did not get the attention they deserved – something which was becoming more and more obvious to the staff in general – and to Seán himself, let it be said.

Even in matters of dress, he had begun to flit, butterfly-like, from one style to another – appearing one day in an old jumper and next day as smartly attired as a bank manager – and much more formally than the Director General himself! Kevin Roche remembers that Seán looked for a while like a retired British colonel, complete with pencil-thin moustache. At other times he might have passed for a Chinese mandarin, with a long, drooping moustache on both sides of his mouth.

Kevin Roche was, at that time, manager of the two Radio Éireann orchestras but every Saturday night he was playing in the Anglesea tennis club with a dance-band known as The Modernaires. When they needed a pianist, Kevin asked Seán to do the job, as he knew he had been a dance-band pianist in Cork. Seán agreed, on one condition – that no one in Radio Éireann would get to know about it. At a certain time every Saturday night, the front line of band musicians would take a break and it was left to Seán on piano, Kevin on bass and George Sterling on drums to provide a session of South American music for the dancers. As Seán and Kevin both knew the classical repertoire, it often happened that the music of famous composers would appear in unexpected rumba and samba arrangements. It did not matter to the drummer what music they played – he would joyfully give it an authentic South American beat. Even after Seán had left Radio Éireann, Kevin rang him urgently about providing a quarter of an hour session of piano jazz. Ó Riada, who was at the time in the Abbey Theatre, said he would only do it using a false name, so they settled on the name Bill Robinson, and no one ever discovered who the excellent jazz pianist Robinson really was!

Seán received encouragement and inspiration from the Hungarian conductor, Tibor Paul, who was working for Radio Éireann. He persuaded Seán to complete his major work, *Nomos 2* in the early 1960s. Paul was Director of Music at the time and conductor of the orchestra, until he was sacked in 1967. Gerard Victory then became Director. Paul conducted the first performance of *Nomos 2* in 1965 and he had a great regard for Ó Riada's talent, though he did not think much of Seán's work methods. I have seen a beautiful letter written by Tibor Paul to Seán in 1967, hoping he might have the chance to shake Ó Riada's hand once more, before he left Ireland.

For much of 1954 and early 1955, letters were piling up on Seán's desk in Radio Éireann. It was clear to both the organisation and to Seán himself that there was no real hope of compromise between Radio Éireann and its Assistant Director of Music. There was considerable tension between Director Fachtna Ó h-Annracháin and Seán in early 1955, as Seán showed signs that he was becoming dissatisfied with the job. Certainly, Radio Éireann was most displeased at his demeanour as Assistant Director of Music and at the fact that the normal duties of his post were being neglected. Those close to him were aware that he was under considerable mental strain – not only in his private life, but in his religious and artistic life as well.

Eventually Seán did not appear at the office and there was a rumour that he was on sick leave. Subsequently, his colleagues understood he had left Radio Éireann and would not return. He had written to Fachtna Ó hAnnracháin in February saying that his main interest was composition and he was not being given time for such work. 'The station cannot claim me body and soul,' he wrote, 'and if it comes to a choice I am afraid I will not be able to continue.'

He took a three-week holiday in March and went to France. It became known that he had gone there to seek work as a musician, leaving Ruth and their baby son Peadar behind in Dublin. In the previous year he had played piano on French radio (RDF). The programme was titled: *Solistes Oeuvres pour piano* (John Reidy). The programme note said he played *Sonatine* and *Cinq Epigrammes*. The date was 8 October 1954. He obviously expected to obtain work there as a musician.

He wrote to Radio Éireann saying that he wished to resign his post, with effect from 22 March 1955. He did play piano at least once on Radio Paris and later claimed to have received an offer of a conductorship in Saigon, as no French conductor wished to go there since France was at war in Vietnam. And it seems Seán was not keen to go either!

Little is known about Seán's Paris sojourn. Names like Messiaen and Schmitt were often mentioned, as people with whom he was in contact, but there is no evidence to support such claims. Ó Riada himself told singer Seán Ó Sé that money was so scarce in Paris that he painted a couple of pictures in the modern style, wore a beret jauntily on his head and tried to sell his creations to buy food, but no one wanted to pay for his art!

Ruth eventually left her young son Peadar with Seán's parents in Cork and went to Paris to look for her husband. She found him after some time, in poor living conditions and in bad health. They contacted Seán's parents in Cork, who posted them money for the return passage to Ireland. It has been suggested that a cheque from Radio Éireann of £80 for his *Slán le Máigh* helped in his return to Ireland.

CHAPTER 5

GAEL LINN

It would be difficult to overestimate the influence Gael Linn had on Ó Riada and equally, the influence Seán had on the organisation, which was established in 1953 to explore new ways of making Irish a living language in Ireland. The history of both would have been very different if they had not met.

Gael Linn was an organisation that belonged to the people in Ireland and abroad who contributed weekly to the football pool they organised to assist their fund-raising. Gael Linn's *timírí*, or agents, were in every parish in the country, collecting a shilling a week from their members and distributing their winnings to the prizewinners.

The organisation wielded considerable influence in a number of other ways: their weekly radio programme ran for some 27 years on Irish radio until the station ceased broadcasting sponsored programmes. The programme was used to give the results of the pool every week and to advertise the many functions in which Gael Linn was involved. Irish music and songs from the company's catalogue of new recordings were played, so that listeners began to feel that the language was not only growing and developing but was, somehow, more their own than it had been.

The first announcer on the programme was Pádraig Ó Raghallaigh, until he left to go to America. He was followed on the programme by Donncha Ó Míodhcháin and Breandán Ó Dúill. Gene Martin was responsible for sound.

Ó Riada's connection with Gael Linn could be said to have begun even before the organisation was formed. An t-Athair Tadhg Ó Murchú had a habit of giving the committee of *An Chuallacht* (the UCC Irish Society) the names of any former Farranferris students who were coming to attend UCC. That was how Riobárd Mac Górain, who had himself attended University College Cork, first got to know Ó Riada was attending UCC and that he was a musician. Riobárd's sister Lillian, like Ruth Coughlan, attended St Angela's secondary school on Patrick's Hill, where Riobárd often met them, with their other school friends, Paula Prendergast and Florrie Fanning, coming home in the evening.

Riobárd Mac Górain finished his course at UCC in 1951 and returned to Dublin, where his family resided. They were Northerners – the father an army officer from Ballinahinch in County Down and the mother from Glenavy in County Antrim. By the time Ó Riada and MacGórain met in Dublin, Riobárd was working for the new organisation Gael Linn and was editor of the Irish magazine *Comhar*. Seán had been appointed Assistant Director of Music in Radio Éireann.

Ó Riada came to the Gael Linn office, which was then in 44 Kildare Street, looking for the editor of *Comhar*. He wanted to write a few articles in Irish for the magazine, to earn some much-needed extra money. He proposed writing articles on music and Riobárd exercised his right to give an advance payment, as soon as he was satisfied that the articles would eventually arrive. The fee was around £2 an article and two or three by Seán appeared subsequently in *Comhar*, but under a pen-name: it was clear that the author, while he undoubtedly knew his subject, was not yet completely fluent in Irish.

At first, Ó Riada and MacGórain spoke mostly in English but as time went on, the atmosphere of the Gael Linn office had its own influence on Seán and later conversations were always in Irish. It was not that any pressure was exerted on Ó Riada – rather that his own life was moving more and more towards Irish, especially at home. Seán and Riobárd discussed all the topics that friends would: Riobárd learned that Seán was a composer of music in the modern idiom but he did not find out until much later that Ó Riada had an interest in Irish traditional music.

Ó Riada had, by this time, already started on the road that was to lead him to participation in a truly Irish way of life – what he himself termed *An Saol Gaelach*. Riobárd discovered that Seán had attended Gael Linn's special nights in the Damer Theatre, where singers and musicians from the Gaeltacht would perform. No doubt, these included some from Cúil Aodha, where Seán and his family were eventually to take up residence in the 1960s. He was very interested in drama in Irish at the Damer and, of course, at the Abbey, where he was by now employed as Director of Music.

When Gael Linn published their first 78 rpm records, Seán asked Riobárd for copies and that was Riobárd's first idea that Ó Riada was interested in traditional music. Riobárd knew from the poet Tom Kinsella of Ó Riada's interest in ballads and had heard his name mentioned in connection with the *Wexford Carol*. Tom and Riobárd had been friends since they shared a bench in O'Connell's School in Dublin, where Tom wrote articles for a school magazine, *An Glaoch*, that Riobárd produced. Tom and Seán had by this time become good friends, with a high regard for each other.

Another important step in Seán's path towards *An Saol Gaelach* was his first visit to the Kerry Gaeltacht in the late 1950s. An t-Athair Tadhg had invited Seán to come and stay at the *bothán*, which surprised Seán as his relationship with the priest at Farranferris had not always been smooth. Tom Kinsella and his wife joined the Ó Riadas in Kerry. It is clear that Seán was impressed by what he found in Kerry in

1959. For the first time in his life he experienced the Irish language and an Irish way of life, in their natural surroundings. It was there he first met the singer Seán de h-Óra, who was to have a considerable influence on him, and there too he met the ordinary people of the area, particularly those who frequented Dónal Ó Cathain's pub in Ballyferriter, where singers and musicians congregated in the evenings.

On his return to Dublin, Ó Riada was full of enthusiasm for the Kerry Gaeltacht and the two very special singers he had met there – Seán de h-Óra and Gerry Ó Flatharta. He wanted Gael Linn to record them and the pair were brought to Dublin at the time of the 1959 All-Ireland Football Final, when a song from each of them was recorded. Ó Riada was in the studio as producer, though Gael Linn did not really use that title in the early days. Unfortunately, Gerry did not live to hear himself on record. He was drowned while out fishing, just a week after his return to Kerry.

When Gael Linn decided to make their first long-playing record, Mac Góráin asked Ó Riada to be editor/producer of the recording. It contained songs by Tomás Ó Súilleabháin, arranged by Ó Riada, with his piano accompaniment. On the B side the Radio Éireann Light Orchestra played arrangements of Irish airs by various composers, including Ó Riada. The second Gael Linn LP had Pilib Ó Laoghaire's *Cór Cois Laoi* on one side and, on the other, a further series of Irish airs, played by the Light Orchestra.

One of Gael Linn's original aims was to make their own Irish films for public showing. They began in 1956 with films by Colm Ó Laoghaire and Vincent Corcoran: Vincent Mulkerns later replaced Corcoran. These first offerings were three-minute shorts that appeared once a month and, later on, fortnightly. Music for them was composed by Gerard Victory. Sound was by Peter Hunt and Gene Martin, with commentary by Pádraig Ó Raghallaigh and the series had the general title *Amharc Éireann*.

These news films continued to be shown regularly in all the major cinemas until attendances began to drop in the 1960s, due to the advent of television. Gael Linn had originally proposed the series of newsreels in Irish to Bobby McKew, manager of Rank in Ireland. To their surprise, Rank not only agreed to distribute the Gael Linn films in all the major cinemas but they paid well for the privilege. Cameramen for the series were Jim Mulkerns, Nick O'Neill and Val Ennis; Breandán Ó h-Eithir wrote the scripts and Eibhlín Ní Bhriain, Gael Linn Press Officer, kept everyone informed.

With the appearance of the first Irish newsreel to be distributed nationally, film-making in Irish had become a reality. Gael Linn, however, had plans to do much more than short newsreels. Dónal Ó Móráin, who headed the organisation, discovered that there was archive film material available, which might be used to make a major Irish film and he knew the man who could do it – George Morrison. Ó Móráin had known George since their student days in UCD and was aware that he was passionately interested in photography and film. George knew of all the archival material available and had already catalogued it, with a view to using it some day for a film. That was how Gael Linn decided to make a major historical film, with George as director. It was felt there might be sufficient material for a second film also. Gael Linn made the momentous and rather hazardous decision to go ahead with the project, using their own funds exclusively. It was a courageous step for the organisation.

They realised early in the proceedings, that the type of archival film material available would be a major factor in deciding what kind of film would eventually emerge. There were fairly serious lacunae in the material at their disposal, which meant it was a matter for the director to shape the overall film so the original footage fitted comfortably into it. It was soon realised music would have an important and quite novel role to play in the film's dramatic impact.

Riobárd MacGóráin recommended Seán Ó Riada as the film's music composer. Morrison, who had someone else in mind for the job, eventually agreed. Others in Gael Linn were not happy about giving such an important task to someone under 30, particularly a person without much relevant experience. When Seán MacRéamoinn was asked his opinion, he spoke highly of Ó Riada and his work in Radio Éireann, with which MacRéamoinn was familiar. It was agreed there should be a meeting on the project between Morrison and Ó Riada. They got on well and were certain they could do a good job. George spent considerable time explaining his requirements to Seán before showing him any actual archive material, as he wished to have most of it put together first, so Ó Riada would feel the atmosphere of the film before writing any music. In those days, viewing a film in the making was not at all easy. One had to book a commercial cinema for a few hours in the morning and resist the manager's pressure to finish the session as soon as possible, so that his staff could prepare for the normal matinée showing in the afternoon.

Much of the music Ó Riada composed for this film (that became *Mise Éire* in 1959) is not actually on the record that was issued subsequently. The piece he composed for O'Donovan Rossa's funeral, for example, is not there. Gael Linn felt that the music to be put out on record should not be based on nationalistic ballads, which were common at the time, but on the more traditional music and songs. Without interfering unduly with the composer's artistic freedom, Gael Linn did all they could to make this view known to Ó Riada.

When he composed the music, Seán let it be known that he would like to conduct the orchestra for the recording. Many doubted whether he had sufficient experience in such matters, but after some delay it was agreed that he should do it. The recording was made on the Tuesday after the June bank holiday in the Phoenix Hall, with Peter Hunt, assisted by Gene Martin, on sound.

It was the first time anyone had heard the full score and there was general satisfaction with Ó Riada's work. Louis Marcus, who was present, remembers thinking that some of it was reminiscent of a work

Seán had composed shortly before this for the opening of the Cork radio station – *Seoladh na nGamhna*. Whatever mixed feelings Ó Riada might have had about some of his work, he was always proud of his score for *Mise Éire*, though he was sometimes not pleased that many thought it was his only composition. What pleased him even less was that they were convinced the film's main theme, *Róisín Dubh*, was his own composition and not part of the Irish heritage of traditional music.

Another important Gael Linn film director emerged in the 1960s – Louis Marcus, who had been interested in film all his life. He served his apprenticeship in the workshop of the Film Society in Cork, where he got help and inspiration from Seán Hendrick, who was Chairman of the Cork branch of the Society. Louis was often in the company of Cork poet Seán Ó Ríordáin and sculptor Séamus Murphy, the latter and his work being the subject of Louis' first film. He was also one of George Morrison's assistants in the making of both *Mise Éire* and *Saoirse*.

Between the end of the Irish newsreels and the mid-1960s, Marcus made a dozen films for Gael Linn. They included *Rhapsody of a River, An Tine Bheo, Peil, Pobal* and *Christy Ring*. The Company received sponsorship for some from Roinn na Gaeltachta, the Department of Foreign Affairs and Players & Wills (Ireland) Ltd. Gael Linn was certainly fulfilling its early promise.

Riobárd MacGóráin remembered many conversations he had had with Ó Riada in the early days, on national affairs and on the Irish language. One day Seán came into the office with his young son, Peadar, and persuaded Riobárd to go out to a nearby café for a chat, as he wanted to talk in private. He was worried about an article Dónal Ó Móráin had written for a Fine Gael magazine, in which he implied you were a better Irish person if you spoke Irish. Seán could not agree with that thesis and the two friends spent a long time earnestly debating the matter. They agreed eventually that the Irish speaker had something extra – something more fulfilling but that one could still be a full Irish person without the language. Riobárd used the example of music to make the argument: surely a person with something as valuable as music had an advantage over the person without it!

When this was settled, Seán raised the question of his name and which version of it he should append to his music. Riobárd remembers being very careful in presuming to deal with such a private and personal matter as a person's name. He told Seán that, based on his experience of using the Irish form of his own name, he was sure that the name John Reidy on a piece of music, while it would be all right, would not be so simple, rhythmical and native as the name Seán Ó Riada. They did not talk about it after that, but from that day on Seán used the Irish form exclusively.

Soon after this, Ó Riada began to take an interest in the books of the Irish book club, *An Club Leabhar*, that often lay on Riobárd's desk. He would sometimes ask for one on loan and Riobárd was happy to let him have any he wished. Ó Riada was excited by one in particular – *An Duiníneach* – the story of the Irish lexicographer, Dineen, written jointly by Northerner Proinsias Ó Conluain and west Corkman Donncha Ó Céileachair. It was about this time that Seán began to buy the Irish folklore magazine, *Béaloideas*. He became an avid reader of it from then on. Poetry in Irish was his next target. He read poems and learned them: Ruth told how he could often be heard reciting poetry at the top of his voice, seated on the toilet!

When the Ó Riada family had taken up residence in Galloping Green, on the outskirts of Dublin, in Longford Terrace, they were close to the MacGóráin home. One day Ruth, in a very distressed state, met Lillian at the shops. She said Seán had just given her notice that she would have to be fluent in Irish within three months. She had no idea how she was going to set about the task: she only knew, from her knowledge of Seán and his logic, that, sooner or later, she would have to accomplish it. Peadar remembers a summer day when they were sunning themselves in the garden and Seán made his bombshell announcement that the Ó Riadas would henceforth be an Irish-speaking family. Speaking of Seán's logic, he himself was of the opinion that his study of the classics in UCC was very useful to him in personal character-building and enabled him to appreciate clearly beforehand the final outcome of any project he undertook. He saw the conversion of the whole family to Irish as one such project.

The fact that Seán wrote a play with music in 1960, *A Spailpín a Rún*, for the Damer Theatre, is an indication of the mastery of the Irish language that he had achieved by this time. Even in his normal conversation Ó Riada was already beginning to practise something of the beautifully flowing prose of the Kerry poet, Eoghan Rua Ó Súilleabháin, while his intense study of folklore, poetry and prose added depth and polish to his speech. It is easy to see now that he was equipping himself for the new life he would like to live – in a truly Gaelic environment. Even though he was not yet aware of it, he was moving inexorably towards an Irish-speaking Ó Riada family, living in the Gaeltacht.

CHAPTER 6

THE ABBEY THEATRE AND CEOLTÓIRI CUALANN

When Seán returned to Dublin, after his French adventure, he was without work and had very little money. He went into Radio Éireann one day, to collect a fee due to him for musical arrangements he had done, and he spoke to Gerard Victory, who had been in touch with Ernest Blythe of the Abbey Theatre. Victory was debating whether or not he should accept an offer as Director of Music in the Abbey, which Blythe had just made to him, following the recent retirement of Éamonn Ó Gallchobhair. Gerard was fairly certain he would not take the job but wanted to have Ó Riada's opinion on the matter. Seán warned him not to even think of accepting, as the job was beneath him and not suitable for a true artist like Victory. Gerard was surprised to hear later that Seán had gone straight over to see Blythe in the Abbey, seeking the post for himself. He obtained it and, as a result, the Ó Riada family were subsequently better off financially, though the salary of Director of Music in the theatre was not very good. In his spare time, Seán did some music-teaching, to earn a little extra money.

Whatever about financial matters, there were considerable personal advantages in Seán's new job: it left him a lot of free time, which was important on two counts – he could make the acquaintance of other musicians, and had more time for his own musical composition. This was, after all, his stated reason for resigning from Radio Éireann. He certainly did compose some of his best work during his term as Director of Music in the Abbey. The name John Reidy appeared for the first time on an Abbey Theatre programme on 25 July 1955. The Abbey was still playing at the Queen's Theatre, pending, as the programme stated, 'Rebuilding and Enlargement of the Abbey'.

The play on his first night there, produced by Ria Mooney, was the first production of John McCann's *Blood is Thicker than Water,* with orchestra playing Rossini's *Tancredi* as overture, then Strauss' *Die Fledermaus* and, finally, *Ceol Gaodlach* (*sic*) – all under the direction of John Reidy. However, Seán used the Irish form of his name for the annual Christmas pantomime from 1955 onwards. The pantomime that year was *Ulysses agus Penelope*, with Rae Mac An Ailí and Máire Ní Dhomhnaill in the leading roles. Apart from *Geamaireacht na Nollag* (pantomime) references, the name Seán Ó Riada did not appear on any other Abbey Theatre programme until 11 July 1960, when the play was Louis D'Alton's *The Money Doesn't Matter*, produced by Ria Mooney, with setting by Tomás Mac Anna. The name Seán Ó Riada appeared on every programme until 26 November 1962 – Seán's last night as Director of Music. The play on that evening was John B. Keane's *Hut 42*, produced by Proinnsias MacDiarmada, with setting by Tomás Mac Anna. Seán then left both The Abbey and Dublin and went west to Kerry. He was credited, though, on the subsequent Christmas pantomime, *An Claíomh Soluis*, for both music and script.

Ó Riada followed a line of well-known musicians as Director of Music in the Abbey. These included Arthur Darley, John F. Larchet and Éamonn Ó Gallchobhair, the latter having retired in May 1955, just before Seán took up the post. His duties were to conduct a small orchestra of four or five players for an overture (if required), interval music and the national anthem at the end of the performance. Seán would play piano and conduct the small orchestra for plays: he had a larger orchestra for opera, plays with music, or pantomime.

During Seán's years in the Abbey, Tomás Mac Anna was Director of the Christmas pantomime. The pair had been friends before this period and co-operated in scriptwriting for the shows, especially after their success with *An Crúiscín Lán* in 1956. They had considerable regard for each other's talent and Tomás always maintained that Seán was capable of writing a first-class opera, given the chance. Ó Riada composed much for music-drama in the period, this being one of his duties as Director of Music. He produced a score for Máiréad Ní Ghráda's *Súgán Sneachta* and *Úll Glas Oíche Shamhna*, as well as for Seán Ó Tuama's *Gunna Cam agus Slabhra Óir*. He also conducted two Gerard Victory operas, *Iomrall Aithne* and *An Fear a Phós Balbhán*, in August 1956.

Even though Seán was no longer an employee of Radio Éireann, he had many scripts accepted by the station during his Abbey years. They included some on classical music analysis, some on jazz, a few on music of other countries and book reviews. The result was that he was still frequently seen in the studios, recording illustrated programmes such as *Great Composers, Their Kind of Music, Making Music,* and *How a Tune is Made.*

Perhaps his most memorable work for the Abbey Theatre in this period was the music he composed for Bryan McMahon's *Song of the Anvil (The Golden Folk).* The play called for Wren Boys on stage, Peadar Lamb, on bodhrán, being one of them. Seán and Bryan decided that the normal Abbey Theatre musicians would not be suitable for the new drama, which would require something more traditional. They brought together a new traditional group that included Paddy Maloney, Éamonn de Buitléar, Michael Tubridy, Seán Potts, Martin Fay (one of the regular Abbey Theatre musicians) and Ronnie McShane, who was already employed by the Theatre to look after stage and sound effects. Ronnie and Seán were to influence one another greatly.

When *Song of the Anvil* had finished its run in the theatre, the band stayed together and continued to practise in Seán's house in Galloping Green. They made their debut in concert at the Shelbourne Hotel, as part of the Dublin Theatre Festival in 1961, having played a radio series for a year, under the title, *Reacaireacht an Riadaigh*.

By this time, Seán's name was everywhere after the success of his music for the film *Mise Éire* in 1959.

When the theme tune from *Mise Éire* was at the height of its popularity, Ray MacAnally asked Ronnie if he had a copy of the record, as he wanted to play a trick on Seán. Ray told Ronnie he intended to come on stage in the middle of the pantomime, announce the name Seán Ó Riada and have the spotlights turned on Seán in the pit. Ronnie had some misgivings about how Ó Riada would take it, but Ray told him not to worry, as he himself would accept the responsibility. It all happened as they had planned and Seán appeared to take it well when the spotlight was turned on him, but it was a different matter when he went backstage later. He berated Ray furiously and refused to speak to him for some time.

Ronnie remembers Ó Riada teaching him how to master various rhythms on the bones. He might have to keep repeating 'Daddy, Mammy, Daddy, Mammy' to himself as he played, or else sing a few lines of a song Seán had taught him, to illustrate a particular rhythm. He remembers Seán's infinite patience in these matters, not only with Ronnie himself, but with other musicians and actors in the Christmas pantomimes. Nevertheless, Ó Riada always liked to get his own way when working with musicians, but if members of the band opposed his way and recommended an alternative, he would leave them to sit by himself, deep in thought and usually return, to say: 'All right, have it your way.'

Éamonn de Buitléar was working in Healy's shop in Dame street, when he first met Ó Riada. Healy's was considered a fairly upper-class establishment that dealt in sporting guns and fishing gear. Seán came in one day, looking for a gun. Though he was dressed like a country gentleman, Éamonn recognised him straightaway, but did not let Seán know this.

He showed Ó Riada a few guns and Seán eventually purchased a two-barrelled Webley & Scott. He did not have enough money to pay for it, so it was arranged that he should get it on hire-purchase, at a fixed amount every month. To further delay his acquisition, he was obliged to go to a Garda station for a licence before he could take the gun home. When Seán signed his name to the hire-purchase agreement, Éamonn asked him if he was the same Ó Riada that had been playing on radio that morning. This led to a discussion on musical matters. Éamonn said he held strong opinions on music and Seán claimed to have some as well. The pair subsequently embarked on a series of fishing expeditions together.

Éamonn and his wife Lally lived very close to the Dargle river at the time and she remembers Seán's first visit to their home to meet Éamonn for a day's fishing. Lally was impressed by his height, and dress style – particularly his hat and houndstooth jacket, which was very much in fashion. At first, Seán was practising fly-casting in their hall, before proceeding to the back-door for earnest practice on the river but without much success. Éamonn remembers being on the riverbank with him at other times, side by side, concentrating on fishing. Éamonn, who was a seasoned fisherman, pretended not to notice that Seán's fly was more often entangled in the branches behind him than floating gently on the water in front. I can guarantee, having seen Seán casting on the Sullán river in Cúil Aodha, many years later, that Éamonn's lessons bore fruit eventually!

Éamonn remembers they often spoke about music on these occasions. Seán told him he lived in Galloping Green and that he wanted to get a group of musicians together to play for a special project. Éamonn mentioned names Ó Riada did not know, including Seán Potts, John Kelly and Sonny Brogan. They were invited out to Seán's

Ceoltóirí Cualann at an informal rehearsal in the Mansion House, Dublin in the early days of the group. Back row, left to right, John Kelly, Sonny Brogan on whistle, Seán Ó Riada, Ronnie McShane, Seán Potts. Front row, left to right, Michael Tubridy, Éamonn de Buitléar, Paddy Moloney, Martin Fay.

house and were joined by others, including Willie Clancy, Garech de Brún, Ciarán MacMathúna, Gene Martin, Peter Hunt and many more.

Seán wanted a group that would bring the arts together, so that music, poetry, song and dance would intermingle at a single session. Éamonn spoke of another occasion, much later of course, when Ó Riada asked him to send out written invitations to every Government minister, asking them to come to a very special night that was to take place in the Shelbourne Hotel. It was a big performance by the new group, Ceoltóirí Cualann, at the Dublin Theatre Festival Club in 1961. What surprised Éamonn was that most of the government ministers turned up and everyone had a great time. In preparation for that concert, the group had a lot of work to do. Most of the members could not read music, but, as we have already seen, Seán had his own ways of getting around this difficulty. Éamonn, who sometimes played bodhrán, remembers a particular rhythm he could not master. Seán told him not to worry, as he would write it out for him – which he did. Éamonn read and memorised his 'music', which was:

Ham, butter and eggs,
Ham, butter and eggs,
Ham, butter and rasher and sausages,
Ham, butter and eggs.

Ceoltóirí Cualann had first made the acquaintance of singer Seán Ó Sé as a result of accompanying him on the famous record, *An Poc Ar Buile*. Seán Ó Sé became vitally important in the advancement of Ceoltoiri Cualann.

Éamonn de Buitléar spoke of the friendship between Ó Riada and Thomas Kinsella, the poet, in those days. In this context, Éamonn remembers Seán, who was always short of money, regularly visiting Healy's shop. Ó Riada earned £11 a week at the Abbey, but he would pretend to Ruth he only got ten, so that he'd have a pound to himself to spend on his beloved cigars. Lally Lamb's memory is that Ruth had to manage the household, food and all, on eight pounds a week.

Nevertheless, Seán came into the shop to buy a Webley air-pistol. Éamonn pointed out that they were very expensive (they were over £7 at the time): nothing would do Seán but the Webley. 'What, in God's name, do you want it for?' asked Éamonn. 'I'll tell you,' said Ó Riada: 'I want it for killing mice. They keep running up and down the dresser at home, when myself and Tom are trying to have a chat, late at night. So there you are!' Éamonn sold him the pistol and heard no more, for a long time – either about the gun or the mice!

The radio programme *Reacaireacht an Riadaigh* continued throughout this period. Darach Ó Cathain was singer with the group – a man for whom Ó Riada had a very high regard. Once, when they had finished recording *Amhrán an Tae* for Gael Linn, Darach turned

Seán Ó Riada and Ceoltóirí Cualann, with Seán Ó Sé singing,
playing at the Peadar Ó Dóirnín memorial concert
in the Gaeity Theatre, Dublin in 1969.

to Éamonn and said: 'Oh, my God, I left out the second part of the music', John Kelly agreed. 'There's no turn in it – the turn is missing'. Darach, as a fine traditional singer, was unique – a person who would always go his own way.

When *Fleadh Cheoil an Radio* began, Ó Riada wanted to arrange music for voice, harpsichord and Ceoltóirí Cualannn. Seán Ó Sé was his choice of singer for that combination, with himself on harpsichord, so that he could more or less direct affairs from his position at the keyboard.

Ó Riada had already deserted the bodhrán at this stage in favour of the harpsichord. Éamonn thought it had something to do with an element of competition that was growing between Ó Riada and Paddy Maloney. Though Seán had at first given the pipes a special place in his arrangements for the group, it was clear that he intended in future to hold a tighter rein on affairs, from his position at the keyboard, than he would have had if he were still playing bodhrán.

Éamonn commented on the fact that Seán was not too fluent in Irish when they first met. English was their most usual means of communication then, so that, in the early *Reacaireacht an Riadaigh* programmes, Ó Riada did not attempt to read the Irish pieces from the script but left that to Niall Tóibín. However, in the programmes subsequent to Seán's Kerry sojourn, he would read such items himself, with a fine Kerry accent. In later years this was transformed into a Cork accent, when the family went to live in Cúil Aodha. Many people were surprised, at the time, that Seán picked up such fluent and excellent Irish in so short a period, but part of the answer is that he was continually studying the language, paying particular attention to every nuance of speech of the native speakers with whom he was in frequent contact.

Fleadh Cheoil an Radio, with storyteller Éamonn Kelly as resident seanchaí, proved a great success. The programme included a series of competitions for various instruments, including violin, flute and singing. At the end of each series, Seán and Ciarán Mac Mathúna would give their adjudication. Seán Keane, now fiddler with The Chieftains, was one of the contestants and won first prize, though he was still very young. Ó Riada invited him to join Ceoltóirí Cualann, which he did. Éamonn remembers Ó Riada telling people after that, 'I have a musician now who looks like a Greek God and plays like an angel'.

One result of Ó Riada moving almost exclusively to harpsichord within the group was the introduction of Peadar Mercier to take his place on bodhrán. Before joining them, Peadar had been on bodhrán in a cabaret group with Paddy Maloney and Seán Potts. When Seán moved to harpsichord, Ceoltóirí Cualann included more music by O'Carolan, the blind Irish harper who was a contemporary of Bach and Handel. They had always played music by the Irish harper, ever since the early Galloping Green days, when Seán would push drawing pins into the hammers of the piano to give it a metallic sound

49

resembling that of a harpsichord. But the drawing pins and piano were now a thing of the past.

When the first Ceoltóirí Cualann record was released, the musicians were extremely dissatisfied that they had not received any cash for their efforts. There was a blazing row between Ó Riada and the players, bringing some of them to vow that they would never again play with him. They claimed the group was finished and Éamonn de Buitléar, fearing they might be right, spoke to Seán about the matter. All Ó Riada would say was, 'If that's the way they want it, so be it. Let's have an end to Ceoltóirí Cualann.'

Éamonn resisted strongly. 'Here is a group which has, or will have, an important place in history – and you're saying, Seán, that it's already finished?' Ó Riada claimed that he did not have any option, if they were looking for money which was not there. Éamonn promised to have further words with the musicians but recommended that, in the meantime, Seán should pay a certain few of them, in the hope that Éamonn might be able to persuade the whole group to come together again. Peace was restored.

Éamonn had an important position in the group, especially after Seán had gone to live in Cúil Aodha. Ó Riada would send either written music or tapes to him in Dublin and Éamonn would book a room in RTÉ, so that they could all rehearse their music, in the Ó Riada arrangement, for the next programme, or programmes, to be recorded for broadcast by RTÉ. It was Éamonn who arranged that Pat Hayes should make a recording of the complete concert they gave in the Gaiety Theatre for the Ó Dóirnín bi-centenary celebrations and it was later issued by Gael Linn on a famous record, *Ó Riada sa Gaiety*. It was intended that the same thing should be done in Cork City Hall for the O'Carolan concert which, though no one knew it at the time, was to be the last concert by Ceoltóirí Cualann. It transpired that the music, for various reasons, did not turn out to be suitable for a stereo recording, notwithstanding the best efforts of Pat Hayes and Éamonn.

However, it did appear in mono on a subsequent record, entitled simply, *Ó Riada*.

After the publication of *Hercules Dux Ferrariae*, Ó Riada announced in a radio interview on RTÉ that Ceoltóirí Cualann was finished as a group and that he was considering the formation of a band of another kind. Éamonn remembers being in a discussion in the Shelbourne Hotel about the proposed new group, with Ó Riada and Len Clifford. The three were enthusiastic about the project, but, not long afterwards, Seán went into hospital.

But to go back, for a while, to happier days – Seán once told Ceoltóirí Cualann that they might be in line for providing the soundtrack for the film, *Playboy of the Western World*, but that the commission had not yet been awarded to anyone. Seán wanted the job but did not know if he had a chance. However, he sent Ronnie McShane out to Galloping Green, to convert the room downstairs into what would pass for a country kitchen. Seán himself was going to the airport to meet the film's directors, who were due to arrive from England. The plan was to bring them directly to the house where, as soon as they heard a loud knock on the front door, Ceoltóirí Cualann would start playing spirited music to welcome the visitors. Some of the players remember being almost blinded by smoke from the big fire Ronnie had lit but they were obliged to keep playing high-speed music as instructed. Their 'wild' music penetrated, of course, through the floorboards to the room above, where Seán and the visitors were drinking wine. They were to have a meal, after which Seán would bring them downstairs, but instead of that, he escorted them down before dinner. The smoke was so thick by now they could only barely see either the musicians or the room. But it didn't seem to matter: everyone was happy and the music did not stop.

Upstairs, the Webley pistol had been left casually on display on the mantlepiece, with a box of ammunition beside it, half-opened, as if the gun was frequently in use – especially since there were two fine cock-pheasants on the table for dinner. But the man of the house had purchased them dearly from a shop in Moore Street! The music continued unabated until Seán came down to them, while Ruth was pouring coffee for the visitors. 'We have it, lads, we have the job! It's in the bag.'

They were all delighted. The directors came down again and it was only then that the music and drinking began in earnest.

Lally Lamb de Buitléar remembers babysitting for the Ó Riadas after Seán had made friends with Éamonn. On the first night, she got a lift to Galloping Green from Peter Hunt and his wife, who were going out for the evening with Ruth. Before they left, Ruth gave Lally all the necessary information about the house and the children – in English, of course, as Ruth did not yet speak Irish. The children were attending the Irish-speaking school, Scoil Lorcáin and Peadar was eight or nine years old at the time and speaking Connemara Irish, as Lally herself did. They got on well together, but she remembers that Peadar could be stubborn if she did not do things in the same way his Mammy did.

Ruth was not keen on housework and much preferred reading a book or going out with friends. Seán had written out a timetable for her, as he was often absent during the day and would be working in the Abbey Theatre in the evening. On this timetable, Seán had pencilled in the name of a man for her – for every night in the week! They were all his friends and included Tom Kinsella, Ciarán MacMathúna, Seán Lucy, Peter Hunt and Seán MacRéamoinn. If Ruth wished to go out for a drink or to the pictures, all she had to do was phone the appointed person. All Seán's friends were fond of Ruth and held her in high esteem.

CHAPTER 7

T RUE   L OVE   IN   H ARD   T IMES

The Ó Riada family during the early Abbey Theatre days were not well off. This is made clear in a number of letters Ruth wrote in 1957, during a single week that Seán was working as an adjudicator at a Feis in Dungannon. Losing a ten-shilling note was a major tragedy where she told Seán of her joy at finding it because the family could then eat once more.

Perhaps more than anything else, the letters show Ruth's great love for her husband and her extreme loneliness at being without him, even for a week. Each note speaks of counting the days until he would return by train on Sunday. The letters clearly meant a lot to Seán, for he kept each one of the four for the rest of his life. They are addressed to: John Reidy B. Mus., McAleer's Hotel, Market Square, Dungannon, Co. Tyrone. They were posted in Blackrock and Dún Laoire in May 1957. Here are extracts from some of them:

My dear John,
I was very happy to get your letter this morning. But it made me feel guilty about the letter you got this morning. I really felt sick when I was writing it and I'm sure it was very depressing for you.

However, I'll try and make up for it today ...

In bed I froze. I had a bottle, but it made no difference: I kept waking up cold and wishing you were there. And last night was even worse. I had my dressing gown and your gabardine over me and still couldn't get warm. This morning Rachel's cot collapsed and I took them both into bed with me, to make the interesting discovery that Rachel is like a little atomic pile of heat and likes nothing better than to bury it in someone else's body. She doesn't mind about smothering. So you can guess what is going to keep me warm tonight ... Peachy is like an ice-cube baby on the other hand and persists in throwing back the clothes. So he sleeps alone. They seem to think you are in another room and Peachy and I have a fearful silent struggle every time we lay the table, as he wants to put out forks and spoons for Dada and John. They look into the bed expectantly in the morning but don't howl upon not seeing you. I think, however, that Peter is secretly beginning to be upset by it, because he said something about you when I put him to bed just now and his face was worried. They probably haven't realised it yet.

I sat with Mrs Boylan last night as it wasn't worthwhile lighting the fire so late up here. She says that if you meet Father Moore of Moy tell him that David Chapman is being ordained in September: our Mrs Cullen is very well-known around there.

I took the children up to Dún Laoire this morning and we had stew for lunch, but I feel like eating sweets or something, but can't waste money on them. It sounds as if Dungannon is every bit as bad as I supposed. Your letter was wonderfully descriptive. What gets me down is the boredom: I'm bored stiff. I'm going to take them off for a walk later on (they are in bed now) and then I have to get through another evening of boredom.

Communion of the intellect through books is not enough without hope of a break. I suppose you are nearly glad to get to the

Feis Hall after the boredom of your room and the town. I have been thinking that we should have a day out on Monday ...

Have you any idea of train times on Sunday? I daresay it's superfluous to enjoin you to leap on the first available means of escape. I'll keep dinner whatever time it is and we can open a bottle. Mrs Boylan has been very good to me. She misses you too. There has been no mail and I have met no one and heard nothing ... Tomorrow is halfway. I never knew a week could be so long. Do you want me to send some escapist literature? I could dig round. I'm looking forward to the phone-call tonight. On Friday I shall have to take R and P into town to collect the pay.

There has been no receipt yet from the bank ... I will give you the list in a later letter. I must go now and post this. The collection down here is at 3.45. I am constantly looking at the clock these days.

I love you madly and I think Sunday will never come. The nights are the worst. I can't sleep. If Rachel works out I'll send her to you for the second half of the week. Please eat enough to keep you alive until Sunday.

Love, Ruth

P.S. I listened to that concert of Irish music on Sunday, but they didn't play any of yours.

The first few pages of the next letter, marked Wednesday, are scribbled in red.

My dear John,

First of all I must tell you that you are wonderful. How you can exist in that dreary northern town I don't know. You must have great resources and capacities and whatnot. I was dreaming about you all night and missing you in my sleep. I had Rachel in with me and she was probably the cause of my dreams, for I was warm at last and felt a human warmth beside me, so I could indulge in spiritual missing as well, as opposed to physical missing, the two nights previously.

After I posted your letter yesterday and came in and got the children ready to go out, I discovered that I had lost ten shillings – my last penny. I spent feverish hours looking for it, punctuated by doorbells and phone calls for Mrs B. I eventually found it in the back at 5.15pm. Since P and R were still champing in the front hall, all dressed to brave the elements, I had to go out. Now I had said, more or less prattling, earlier on, that I would bring them down to see the boats, but ...

Later:

We came home and I started to make chocolate cakes and you phoned. I was glad to hear your voice, but you didn't say much. Phones are so unsatisfactory. You sound doubtful about Sunday. For God's sake, don't tell me you aren't coming home! Please assure me.

Shortly after you, McCann phoned about the violinist for *Pósadh*, next week and said that 'the lady John had in mind', whom I take to be the estimable Miss Hayes, will not be available to do it, as she will be missing some nights. He had been looking for you on Monday night and wanted to know if you had done anything further. I said I thought not and he said he'd go ahead and get someone himself – some trad fiddler they had before. So I said if he had any difficulty to let me know and he said OK ...

So, after that, I made ham sandwiches (all this surplus food, in case you are wondering, being what I wouldn't face for Monday's lunch – ham and eggs, etc.) and we had tea, but Peter fiddled with the gas tap and the oven went out in the middle of cooking the cakes and I didn't know about it – so, as you can imagine, the cakes weren't the best ever. They were still edible though.

After that I got fed up and threw them into bed without ceremony and retired in here, leaving all, where I read Jeeves and laughed and laughed and smoked and chewed and went to bed at 11, collecting dear Rachel en route. She hated to be disturbed, but approved when she got the general idea. She is fearfully restless in bed and grunts and moans a lot. At one stage, I woke up to find my head hanging out over the side, while Rachel lay full-length between me and the pillow. I had no idea she was so strong. However, it was better to wake from a kick or a shout, etc., from Rachel than from the cold, as formerly. She also tried to dress me rather early, but if she hadn't been there I probably would have stayed in bed until all hours.

This morning we didn't go out, as I had the dinner in, so I mooched around, lighting fires and making beds and watching them get dirty. We had lunch at 12.30. I was going to take them for a walk this afternoon but this bloody rain is a bit off-putting. Owing to my fool's errand on Monday – 2/3 cab, 2/8 refreshments, 3/- Peachy's hair, we are very short of money. I have 8/- odd left but want to get my hair done tomorrow while Mrs McConville is here and I won't borrow from Mrs B., as I don't want to louse-up next week's pay. So, however bad your lunch is tomorrow, you can think of us munching potatoes and drinking milk and chewing each other through the afternoon ...

In the same envelope as the above, in a child's handwriting, was the following:

Dear John,
You are missing all the boats. Come home at once, as Ruth is very mean about taking me down.
    Love, Peachy

Below the signature was the following:
P.S. Don't bother.
Rachel.
The third letter, probably written on the Thursday, is shorter:

My dear John,
I was glad to see by your letter that you are in a better frame of mind. The adjudicating doesn't seem to be driving you as mad as I thought. This is going to be a short letter, as I'm in a hurry ...

I overslept this morning (or rather Rachel fiddled with the alarm clock so that it was an hour slow).

So I rushed out of bed and out without even a cup of tea. My hair appointment was for 10.30. I got there 10.45 but he wasn't busy. He was the first to give me the glad news that the budget is a stinker – flour and butter subsidies off, cigs up 2d, beer 1d, petrol 6d (which means bus-fares) and diesel oil (which means train-fares): children's allowance is 4/6 – great, isn't it?

The gas has gone and I don't know how I'll clean those two. I know you are very good and like to bring things home, but please don't spend much. Don't get either the powder or the foundation cream. I will write you a long letter tonight. I sat with Mrs Boylan last night after 9 and let my fire out. Please understand my predicament and don't reply a short letter to this. I am glad you are such a success, but next time I'm going with you. Write or phone me if you are short. Only two more days to go. I wish I knew what time you are coming Sunday so I could look forward to it. I suppose you won't get this until afternoon too. The collections round here are very bad.

I love you madly.
Ruth

The final letter is scribbled on foolscap paper with an embossed harp heading on each page:

Dear John,

I'm fearfully tired. I have just come in from collecting your pay and as I had to take them with me, it was a ghastly strain – and they kept losing shoes and money and squirming and crying and I felt like a drop underprivileged – especially since the ladders in my stockings are now about three inches wide and there is no possibility they will be unnoticed. But I bought a pair at 6/11 at Clery's just now, so at least you won't be ashamed of me on Monday.

It was very nice of you to send the 10/- but you shouldn't have. I am terrified you will be short or overdraw from the bank. Anyway, if you hadn't sent it we wouldn't have had anything to eat until now and I probably would have fainted in the bus. As it is, we were able to go in with a belly full of spaghetti – which was some relief. I feel very depressed about the budget – the butter has gone up to 4/4 and the sugar 7 $^1/_2$ and God knows what milk and bread will be. You have to work your head off earning money and then we find ourselves as badly off as ever.

And I have been very lax about keeping to my schedule. When something unexpected, such as Julia or you going away happens, I don't seem able to cope. You must try to help me next week and write out the fixed prices for me. I'm trying again today. I find that if I miss one day in putting down what I got and balancing, I get balled up for the week. My milk bill will be three weeks on Saturday. I got the receipt from the bank this morning. Simmons phoned to say Bob was hysterical about next week's programme. So I said I'd see about it and was going to be panicked into phoning you at lunchtime when I thought of Eric O'Gorman.

I rang and asked for him and he said, abruptly: 'Yes': 'This is Mrs Reidy': 'Oh yes':

'I just want to check if my husband has sent in next week's

programme': … long pause …: 'programme?': 'Music programme
for next week': 'Oh, programme for next week': … long pause …:
'Yes': 'He has?': 'Yes': 'Good – I wanted to check because Mr
Simmons rang me up in a bit of a panic': 'Yes, he's doing, let me
see, an overture and then some selections': 'Oh good, good, thank
you, goodbye'.

Now, of course that could cover any programme for the last
thirty years, but I take it he received news from you in this morning's post and assured Mrs Woods of this when she in turn questioned me as I collected the pay. I told her you were coming back
on Sunday and had called a rehearsal for Monday, so she said fine.
The *Pósadh* fiddler seems to be still somewhat woolly. Simmons
said he'd 'have another go' off May tonight, which seems to indicate McCann hasn't told him he is fixing it up, or rather, that he
is getting Seán Mooney to fix it up. So be prepared to find that
nobody knows anything about it when you arrive in. S. said that
McCann said it must be the same fiddler each night – I suppose
because Rafteri has to synchronise with the fiddler offstage. Hence
the difficulty about getting either Kennedy or Hayes or, I suppose,
Martin. Anyway, you can instruct me on the phone tomorrow, if
you wish. I'll phone Seán Mooney or Simmons tonight and try to
find out where we are. So much for business …

Now, for your letter …

I did get your Tuesday letter and thought I had intimated as
much, but perhaps I didn't. Anyway, I get one every morning and
find them very satisfactory. I see you have a touching confidence
in Simmons. Well, I suppose he knows what he's doing. You
shouldn't take any notice of my bits of bitchiness with regards to
other women - after all, it's feminine nature. I thought, in fact, I
showed remarkable restraint, as I was tempted to suggest the sort
of creams suitable and why, etc., but was too charitable to do so …

I'm sorry you are depressed and having such a struggle with

the audience, but you seem to be able to handle them very well indeed. Isn't it wonderful to think you will be home the day after tomorrow and it will all be part of the past, etc. I must go now. Please let me know what time you are coming back. Write down what you want to say on the phone and I'll do the same, so that we won't waste time. I love you madly and I'll be very nice to you on Sunday.

Love, Ruth

CHAPTER 8

Ó RIADA THE COMPOSER

Being a general biography this is not intended to give a detailed analysis of Seán's compositions. *Seán Ó Riada: A Shaol agus a Shaothar* by Gearóid Mac an Bhua and myself gives such analysis. For various reasons, there is as yet no complete listing of all Ó Riada's compositions – some were either lost or never documented.

His first serious musical output appeared in 1954 and included *Sonatine* and *Eight Preludes*, as well as a setting of Ezra Pound's *Lustra*. However, what may be regarded as his first major composition, and the one that drew the attention of serious musicians and critics, was his *Olynthiac Overture*.

Seán produced the final version of the overture in December 1955, called it *Opus 7* and signed it John Reidy. It received its first performance in 1956.

The *Olynthiac Overture* is scored for full orchestra, with a percussion section of kettle and side-drums, tam-tam and rattle. *Adagio ma non troppo* is the marking of the powerful opening, with full orchestra involved from the first bar. A subsequent falling figure leads to a playful development, where Ó Riada demonstrates his orchestral maturity and skill. Brass and timpani are involved in an impressive interlude that builds up to a martial finale.

It seems that this confident work is the 24-year-old John Reidy saying, 'Listen, I have arrived'. This was the first fruit of his new, relatively relaxed period, as Musical Director with the Abbey Theatre and his more comfortable living quarters in his house in Galloping Green.

Soon after the first performance of the *Olynthiac Overture,* Seán was commissioned by Radio Éireann to write a score for Donal Giltinan's *The Last Troubadour,* a Percy French documentary for radio. He produced a much-admired score of some twenty minutes, for soloists, mixed choir and orchestra.

Nomos No. 1, Hercules Dux Ferrariae, appeared in 1957 and signalled a new Irish voice on the European music scene – one that seemed to be attempting a synthesis of the old and new. This was the first public use of the term *Nomos* to describe an Ó Riada composition. The Greek word *Nomos* means law and it had been used by early Greek composers to describe works which had been composed according to certain laws of composition. Seán used it for his major works in what we may call, for want of a better term, the European idiom.

He followed the example of Josquin de Prés, who had been court musician to the Duke of Ferrara in Italy in the early sixteenth century and who had used the vowels of his patron's name to give him the main theme of a composition. Seán used the same name but in a slightly different order, to give him the solfa names of the theme of his new composition.

From the vowels of *Ferrariae Dux Hercules,* Seán got the tonic-solfa names: re, fa, me, re, ut, re, ut, re. Remembering that 'ut' in medieval times was the equivalent of our 'doh', we see that Seán's theme became, equating doh with the note C; D,F,E,D,C,D,C,D. This is the opening theme and unifying motif of the work, which lasts for under twenty minutes.

Much of *Hercules Dux Ferrariae* is in what was then the very modern Schoenberg twelve-note method of composition, which Seán had analysed in his B. Mus. project in University College Cork, some three years earlier. But his use of it is always governed by his own musical instincts and he uses the notes of the motif described above to provide a kind of tonal base for each movement, something that contradicted the basic tenet of the dodecaphonic method of Schoenberg, which does not allow any single tone to have precedence over the others. There are two different twelve-note tone rows used in the work, which has eight movements.

The last movement is a fugue, based on D, the final note of the theme, with what one might regard in a classical fugue as counter-subject, based on the tone rows. The seriousness and discord of much of the previous movements does not prepare the listener for the ironic twist in the tail that Ó Riada gives us with, of all things, a jig in major tonality. Basically it is a verse answered by a chorus, which is the Josquin theme in a new guise. It is marked Quodlibet – Giga, which I think Seán, with a smile, might have translated as: 'whatever you're having yourself now: how about a jig?'

ORCHESTRAL ARRANGEMENT OF AIRS

Seán produced many arrangements of Irish airs for orchestra, some of which are models for what he was to compose for his later film work.

He was commissioned by Seán Mac Réamoinn to write the music for two radio programmes to celebrate the opening of the Cork radio station in 1958. One was based on a poetic evocation of Cork, written by Robert O'Donoghue, who recalls that the co-operation between himself and Ó Riada, for various reasons, was anything but peacefully productive. Seán Mac Réamoinn's diplomatic skills were severely tested over the period of the programme's preparation but the end result was a considerable success. It was titled *In Praise of Cork*, with verse sequence by O'Donoghue. Music, played by the Radio Éireann Symphony Orchestra, was composed and conducted by John Reidy. Apart from the opening theme of 'The Banks of my own Lovely Lee' and 'Oft in the Stilly Night', which had been played at Terence McSwiney's funeral, the rest of the musical items were original, short compositions by Ó Riada.

The other radio programme, *Clár Geal Mumhan*, in Irish and produced by Aindrias Ó Gallchóir, featured a number of airs on French horn, including the Munster song *Clár Bog Déil*, in an arrangement that was the model for Seán's later use of *Róisín Dubh* in the Gael Linn film *Mise Éire*. It also featured traditional Munster songs and fiddle-music. The opening barántas and some of the poetry was by Seán Ó Ríordáin. There were also poems from various parts of Munster by the Limerick poets of the Maigue, Seán Ó Tuama and An Mangaire Súgach (Aindrias Mac Craith), as well as verse by Donncha Rua Mac Conmara, Eoghan Rua Ó Súilleabháin and Piaras Firtéir. Ó Riada's music was the sensitive link throughout.

Seoladh na nGamhna (The Driving of the Calves) was written in autumn 1959 for Aloys Fleischmann's Cork Symphony Orchestra.

Slán le Máigh is the air of a poem by the Limerick poet, Aindrias Mac Craith, or to give him the pen-name by which he was better known, *An Mangaire Súgach*, since he was a pedlar. He was one of the poets of the Maigue (Filí na Máighe), the other main one being Seán Ó Tuama from Croom, or Cromadh an tSubhachais – Croom of the Sweetness. Seán's fondness for the Maigue poets may have been partly because he spent his early youth in Adare, County Limerick. The air is one of our most beautiful and sits comfortably here in its rich orchestral colouring.

FILM MUSIC
Seán wrote music for a number of films, including *Playboy of the Western World*, *Young Cassidy* and *Kennedy's Ireland*. The music for *The Playboy*, which appeared in 1962, was traditionally based and reflected his involvement with Ceoltóirí Cualann. The commission to write the score for John Ford's film, *Young Cassidy*, must have been

attractive to Ó Riada, since the project involved a short sojourn in Hollywood for the composer before the film appeared in 1965.

Mise Éire (I am Ireland), the first of the three Gael Linn films he wrote scores for, which was premiered in 1959, is certainly the most famous of the three and the one which, as far as the Irish public was concerned, made Ó Riada's name. It was directed by George Morrison and was based on archival footage from the silent era, showing many of the incidents and personalities associated with the 1916 Rising. The music needed to be specially composed to enhance the obvious drama of the various events depicted.

Seán saw it as an opportunity to use Irish traditional song airs in a rich orchestral setting to support and complement the fast-changing film clips of the earlier period. Basically, he used one song for each of the half-dozen sections of the film, beginning with the well-known *Róisín Dubh*, played beautifully on French horn.

Slow drum beats below the '98 air, *Sliabh na mBan* (Mountain of the Women) set the scene for the fourth section, funeral of the Bachelor's Walk victims. The first theme returns for a later section, By O'Donovan Rossa's Graveside. The *Sliabh na mBan* theme returns on oboe for the section, Dublin Devastated, before it is taken up and varied by strings. The *Róisín Dubh* motif is used in the *Asgard* sequence, before the full orchestra makes a final majestic summary of the *Mise Éire* theme.

The film was an instant success and not only did *Róisín Dubh* soon become known as *Mise Éire* but nearly everyone began to believe that the tune had been composed by Seán! He had arranged the score so cleverly that he was able to have a fully ornamented traditional line coming from the orchestra, without changing the basic time-signature of 3/4.

As well as the premiere of *Mise Éire* in 1959, Ó Riada was involved in a major dramatic work for radio, *The Lords and the Bards*, the poetic play by Roibeárd Ó Faracháin, with music by Ó Riada, which was

George Morrison, Dónal Ó Moráin and Seán Ó Riada at the launch of the Gael Linn film Saoirse? *in 1960.*

Ireland's entry that year for the *Prix Italia*. The work, some 50 minutes long, is concerned with Saint Colmcille at Drumceat, defending the poets of Ireland, after he had returned from exile in Scotland. Music is mostly on wind instruments, though piano does make a surprising entry in the Allegro. The text is spoken and chanted, and on occasion given to the choir. There are also considerable orchestral linking sections.

Saoirse? (Freedom?), directed by George Morrison and with music by Ó Riada, was premiered in 1961. The film opens with French horn playing *The Croppy Boy*, which is taken up by strings and leads to *Kelly the boy from Killane*. The dramatic Terence McSwiney funeral sequence is followed by an unusual setting of *Who Fears to Speak?* and to a black-and-tan sequence which creates its threatening atmosphere with minimum musical means. Martial themes lead to trumpet's *Last Post* and a repeat of the opening *Croppy Boy* music. While composing the music for *Saoirse?* in 1960, Seán was also involved in *Spailpín a Rún,* premiered at the Dublin Theatre Festival.

His *Triptyque pour Orchestre Symphonique* dates from this productive period in his life.

An Tine Bheo (The Living Fire), which appeared in the year of the fiftieth anniversary of the Rising, 1966, was directed by Louis Marcus who had worked on *Mise Éire*. This final film of the Gael Linn trilogy, for which Seán Ó Riada composed the music, might be seen as a celebration of the heroes of 1916. For *An Tine Bheo*, Ó Riada moved away from exclusive use of traditional, seán-nós material he had used for *Mise Éire*.

Horn opens with the *Beinsin Luachra* theme and various martial episodes occur throughout the work, including *A Nation Once Again, Who Fears to Speak* and *God Save Ireland*. The Pearse theme is a very moving *Táim-sa im Chodladh* and the Roger Casement theme is a short, understated reference to the song *Lonely Banna Strand*, which, of course, is where Casement came ashore. The air is interesting, as it was not the original air of the song, but one recommended to the two Seáns by Seán Ó Sé's mother, some years before Ó Riada wrote the score for *An Tine Bheo*. It is the air of *The Union of Macroom*, which is very similar to *Down Erin's Lovely Lee*.

At the same time as he was composing the music for *An Tine Bheo*, Ó Riada was working on another orchestral composition for orchestra, *Nomos No. 6*, commissioned by the Belfast Festival. It was to be the latest in the series of *Nomoi*, which included an unfinished *Nomos No. 3* (a trio for flute, viola and bassoon).

PIANO AND ORCHESTRA

Nomos No. 4 for piano concertante and orchestra, while it may seem to resemble *Nomos No.1* in some respects, was a new departure for Ó Riada. The work is not a piano concerto in the romantic mould, with a virtuoso solo part, but rather a co-operative musical journey for piano and orchestra.

Rather than look for a Greek or medieval model, the music of the Indonesian gamelan seems to have given Ó Riada his inspiration. He does not employ the gongs of the gamelan but confines himself to the regular percussion instruments, including bells, vibraphone and xylophone, with piano, to give the exotic sounds he required.

The work is in two movements. In the first, *Andante*, a tone row in crotchets, with an eastern sound, is laid out as a basis for the movement. It is developed in canonic fashion amongst the instruments of the orchestra, resulting in complex harmonic structures. Piano uses chromatic accompaniment below a variation of the tone row, while violins and flutes combine with transposed versions of the row.

The second movement, *Allegro*, uses the original tone row with considerable development.

LITURGICAL COMPOSITIONS

As noted elsewhere, Seán formed a male choir in Cúil Aodha soon after his arrival there in the early 1960s. It was subsequently known as Cór Chúil Aodha and soon began to sing at weekly mass in the local church. It was for them that Seán composed, over a period, the various sections of his first unison mass – one of the earliest vernacular masses in the country. Much of it is traditionally based and proved to be suitable for the choir, most of whom were traditional singers, for whom the ornamentation in many of the liturgical pieces would have been their normal way of singing the seán-nós songs of the area.

Aifreann 1, Seán's first unison mass, The Introit, *Is beannaithe Tigh Dé,* has a slowly stepping chordal accompaniment on organ, with some ornamentation, while *Kyrie* and *Gloria* have simple non-ornamented lines, with one note per syllable above slowly moving block chords. *The Offertory, Ag Críost an Síol* and the *Our Father* are both ornamented in traditional style, while the Communion hymn, *Gile Mo Chroí*, is the prayer by the poet Tadhg Gaelach, set to the air of the traditional song, *Sa Mhainistir Lá*. One of the hymns in the *Aguisín* to the mass is Tomás Rua Ó Súilleabháin's poem, *A Rí an Domhnaigh*, set to a traditional air (*Túirne Mháire / An Brianach Óg*), with frequently varying time-signatures to achieve the flexibility required for the text.

Aifreann 2, Seán's second unison mass, was first performed at Glenstal Abbey in 1970. I was approached some years after Ó Riada's death by Dom Paul McDonnell of Glenstal who wanted to get a score for the mass, that it might be performed again. He had a recording of the first performance, with Seán playing organ, but there was no score. We arranged that Eilís Cranitch and myself would undertake the editing of the mass from the tape. Gael-Linn published it in 1979. At the request of Dom Paul, I composed a Psalm, which he felt was liturgically necessary, as there had not been one sung at the first performance. I eventually produced *Maifead Thú*. The second mass, excellent though it is, has, perhaps, less of a traditional Irish ethos than the first.

Polyphonic Masses – Ó Riada was commissioned by RTE to write two works which were intended to be used on the death of President de Valera. They were *Requiem do Shaighdiúir* and *Aifreann Requiem,* both scored for mixed choir, soloists and organ. The only difference between them was that *Aifreann Requiem* had two additional items, a communion hymn, *Gile mo Chroí,* the same used in Seán's first mass, but set here for soloist and choir, and a recessional using the text *In Paradisum,* set for contralto, choir and organ, with musical references back to the *Introit*. It seems to me that in *Aifreann Requiem,* written at the very end of his life, Seán came nearest to an integration of the European and Irish traditions in his music, particularly in his moving setting of *Gile Mo Chroí*. RTE commissioned two other pieces from him for President de Valera, a *Funeral March* and *Music for Pipes*. The tragic irony is that Seán died before the president.

SETTINGS OF POEMS FOR SOLO VOICE AND PIANO

It should be no surprise that such an outstanding keyboard performer and accompanist as Seán should have produced a number of settings for solo voice and piano. Given his abiding interest in literature it was to be expected that his settings would, as a minimum, provide an empathetic vehicle for the poetry and, in some cases, illuminate the text. Soon after his arrival in Dublin Seán made friends with the poet Thomas Kinsella. It was a friendship that was to last throughout Ó Riada's short life. The two friends collaborated on innovative radio programmes such as *The Cruise of the Bugaboo*, with text by Kinsella and music by Ó Riada.

Among Seán's earliest settings were three poems by Thomas Kinsella – *Night Song 1, Night Song 2* and *Classical*. Each of the two *Night Songs*, with different poetic moods, get appropriate music from Ó Riada.

Seán produced settings for poems by Irish poets, John Montague (*Hill Field*, 1965) and Séamus Heaney (*Lovers on Aran* 1968), as well as a most unusual setting of a German nonsense text (Sekundenzeiger, 1966) by Hans Arp, in memory of Ó Riada's young friend Tara Browne.

Ó Riada's best known settings for voice and piano are the four Hölderlin songs, *In Memoriam Aloys G. Fleischmann*, dedicated to Seán's former organ teacher – father of Professor Fleischmann of University College Cork, who was some years later to recruit Ó Riada into his Department of Music. These four songs, sung by Bernadette Greevy, were issued by Claddagh Records on the record *Vertical Man*, along with *Nomos No. 1*. They are *Die Heimat* (home), *Fragment*, *Hälfte des Lebens* (in the middle of life) and *Zimmern* (a poem by Hölderlin dedicated to his friend Zimmern). Apart from the Hans Arp

Sekundenzeiger mentioned above, the Hölderlin songs are the only German language songs set by Ó Riada.

Seán Ó Riada had studied ancient Greek at school and in his first year at university. It was an interest that was to stay with him throughout his life and inspire some of his best work.

Seán Lucy and Ó Riada spent considerable time reading the ancient Greek classics in translation, as Lucy was doing an MA thesis which included a study of the three Theban plays of Sophocles: *King Oedipus, Oedipus at Colonus* and *Antigone*. Ó Riada was to use quotations from two of the plays, *Oedipus at Colonus* and *Antigone*, in his major work, Nomos 2. The translations for *Nomos 2* were by E.F. Watling.

Ó Riada had an abiding interest in the ancient Greek language and enjoyed reading the plays in their original form. He aspired to setting Greek language texts to music and eventually set five Greek epigrams for voice and guitar in 1958, the year of his *Nomos No. 4*. The work was dedicated to Hans Waldemar Rosen, conductor of the Radio Éireann Singers, who gave the first performance in 1961. *Nomos 2* for baritone solo, choir and orchestra was premiered in 1965.

The Sophocles texts are among the high points of Greek drama, based on the legend of the royal house of Thebes. As in all Greek tragedy the plays in no way resemble the theatre of our day, regarded as entertainment. The Greek plays were specially written for public viewing by huge audiences at important Athenian festivals and Greek drama was concerned with the ritualistic expression of major themes of life, death and fate. The employment of a Chorus commenting on the action of the play, as well as acting a part or parts in the drama, was an essential element in Sophocles' plays. The Chorus in both *King Oedipus* and *Antigone* played the part of Theban elders, while in *Oedipus at Colonus* the Chorus are the elders of Colonus. An important function of their performance was to emphasise both the religious element in the dramatic plot and the moral dilemma of the principal actors.

The pessimism of Sophocles' texts on life, death and fate found an echo in Ó Riada's mind. Though Seán had a sense of humour and a certain flippancy, we know there was another side to his nature – a preoccupation with and a fear of death, ever-present throughout his short life.

The first part of *Nomos 2*, the *Praeludium*, begins with a well-known motif of four notes, used so often by composers of the past as to have become almost a cliché: this motif becomes the first part of a tone-row, which is reversed and inverted and sometimes produces quite a discordant sound, quite in keeping with the tragedy that is to come.

The text used in the first movement is taken from *Antigone*:

Happy are they who know not the taste of evil.
From a house that heaven hath shaken
The curse departs not
But falls upon all of the blood ...
In life and in death is the house of Labdacus stricken ...
Well was it said,
Evil seems good
To him who is doomed to suffer;
And short is the time before that suffering comes.

The second movement begins with a light introduction before the baritone sings his pessimistic, 'Time, time, my friend ...'

OEDIPUS:
Time, Time, my friend,
Makes havoc everywhere; he is invincible.
Only the gods have ageless and deathless life;
All else must perish. The sap of earth dries up,
Flesh dies, and while faith withers falsehood blooms.

The spirit is not constant from friend to friend,
From city to city, it changes, soon or late;
Joy turns to sorrow, and turns again to joy.

Between you and Thebes the sky is fair; but Time
Has many and many a night and day to run
On his uncounted course; in one of these
Some little rift will come, and the sword's point
Will make short work of this day's harmony.
Then my cold body in its secret sleep
Shall drink hot blood.

The third movement, marked Scherzo, is an altogether happier movement, using various quotations from the following:

CHORUS:
Of Happiness the crown
And chiefest part
Is wisdom, and to hold
The gods in awe.
This is the law
That, seeing the stricken heart
Of pride brought down,
We learn when we are old.

The music quotes the medieval theme, *L'Homme Armé*, much used in times past in many compositions, including mass-settings. It is here given its authentic musical sound on brass, before being developed by the orchestra.

The fourth movement is written for solo baritone and harpsichord. The use of harpsichord should not surprise those who know Seán's penchant for the instrument in his later work.

CHORUS:
Show me the man who asks an over-abundant share
Of life, in love with more, and ill content
With less, and I will show you one in love
With foolishness.
In the accumulation of many years
Pain is in plenty, and joy not anywhere
When life is over-spent,
And at the last there is the same release
When Death appears,
Unheralded by music, dance, or song,
To give us peace ...

This is the work that Seán submitted to the National University of
Ireland for the degree of D. Mus. The D. Mus was refused, the main
reason being the use of classical quotations and their treatment in the
final movement. Seán was displeased when Professor Fleischmann told
him this, so the professor consulted a further outside authority, who
gave him the same opinion.

After a short introduction, based on earlier sections of the work,
one is surprised to hear Brahms' St Anthony Chorale from the wood-
wind of the orchestra. A dissonant chord interjects and suddenly the
choir is singing, 'Happy are they who know not the taste of evil'. Then
follows the opening of Mozart's *G minor Symphony No. 40*, which is
rejected in just the same manner.

Even Beethoven is not spared and we hear part of the slow movement of his seventh symphony. This was a particular favourite of
Seán's and he used to quote it in his class as an example of two things
– firstly, as an impressive melody which repeats the same note many
times and yet does not bore and secondly, as an example of the use of
the metrical unit, the spondee. All his classical quotations in this *Finale
of Nomos 2* may be regarded as variations of the spondee.

After this surprising opening, tentative percussion seems to lead us towards a new musical experience which has left the classical field and is moving into another dimension, with wordless sounds from choir adding to the tension of the development. Brass heralds pizzicato strings and then gives the earlier theme to which baritone sings:

Our fires, our sacrifices and our prayers the gods abominate.
How can the birds give any other than ill-omened voices?

The choir then takes up the final statement:

CHORUS:
This is the end of tears:
No more lament.
Through all the years
Immutable stands this event.

Brass completes this important work with a re-statement of the medieval theme heard at the beginning. The last word musically is a complete discord which rises powerfully from the lowest notes, up through the orchestra.

THE FIVE GREEK EPIGRAMS
The gentleness of Seán's setting of the Five Greek Epigrams for choir, flute and guitar is in complete contrast to the powerful solemnity of *Nomos No. 2*. These poems from the Greek anthology speak to us of nature and of the idyllic life. In many ways, the epigrams here are a forerunner of the pastoral poetry of Europe in much later times.

1. The first epigram is by Agathias Scholasticus, a Christian who lived in Byzantium in the sixth century AD. It is clearly in praise of the sea, with good advice for the sailor who wishes to sail safely. The mood of

serenity and peace is established by the choir, with a very simple diatonic accompaniment from flute and guitar.

> The deep lies becalmed and blue;
> for no gale whitens the waves,
> ruffling them to a ripple,
> and no longer do the seas break round the rocks,
> retiring again to be absorbed in the depth.
> The Zephyrs blow and the swallow twitters
> round the straw-glued chamber she has built.
> Take courage, thou sailor of experience,
> whether thou journeyest to the Syrtis
> or to the beach of Sicily.
> Only by the altar of Priapus of the harbour
> burn a scarus of ruddy gurnards.

2. The second epigram was composed in the third century BC by Leonidas from Sicily. In it the noisy cicada speaks and Ó Riada lets us hear it through the flute, with guitar accompaniment.

> Not only in the high branches of the trees
> Would you see me, singing sweet in the heat of the day
> Making music for the traveller, as I drink the fresh dew.
> You will see me sit like the sword of the goddess Athena:
> I give her special honour, for I am a musician
> And Athena created the flute!

3. Anacreon, who lived in the fifth century BC, is the composer of the next epigram. His hedonistic verse was to influence subsequent poetry for a long time. Like all the best epigrams, it is short and to the point. Guitar accompanies tenor in the opening phrase, with a repetitive triplet figure supporting the opening words:

I do not care about the wealth of Gyges, lord of Sardis:
I have never envied him, and I have no grudge against tyrants.
I care about drenching my beard with perfumes,
I care about garlanding my head with roses;

4. Theocritus, the composer of the following epigram, was born in Syracuse in Sicily in the third century BC, but spent much of his life in Egypt. In this epigram the musician Xenocles is making a presentation to the Muses in thanksgiving for the fame that his art has gained him and to assure them he does not forget. The opening, for sopranos and altos, is not unlike the opening of the previous epigram, with the three quavers replaced here by three crotchets, and a different time-signature. The setting is of extreme simplicity, with only a few repetitions of phrases of the text. Accompaniment is by guitar at first, with later decorative passages on flute.

The musician Xenocles dedicated this stone monument
To the nine Muses as a token of thanks
For all the fame he got from his art
And he does not forget them for it.

5. Antiphilos, who lived in the first century AD returns to the theme of the sea in this last epigram. This return to the subject of the opening Agathias epigram gives the work an added unity.

PRAYER FOR A CALM SEA-PASSAGE
Blest god of the harbour, ship-ruler,
send a gentle breeze as far as Triton's realm;
and you, who own the shore's extremity,
make safe the voyage to the Pythian shrine.
From there, if we singers all are dear to Phoebus,
I shall sail heartened by a fair-blowing west wind.

CHAPTER 9

Ó RIADA AND IRISH TRADITIONAL MUSIC

It is claimed by many that Seán Ó Riada changed Irish traditional music. This is certainly not a claim that Seán would have made: he always emphasised the conservative nature of the Irish tradition and when he sought performers to illustrate his various radio and television programmes, he went to the older performers with established ways of playing or singing. His aim was to let people hear how real traditional music, played by the best players, sounded and to set a standard by which traditional performance could be judged. He gave players a language in which they could discuss their own music.

One should remember that Seán had traditional music on both sides of his family tree, even though it only became an important part of his life in his late twenties. There is no evidence that he played it at all during his days in University College Cork, though Seán Lucy claimed that Ó Riada was very interested in Irish song. His main musical pastimes there, at least in his own free time, were, as already mentioned, either jazz, pop or South American style, with local bands or at student functions.

It seems that Seán's journey throughout Ireland, looking for performers to illustrate his radio and television programmes, was a study of the current state of Irish music. Seán's keen analytical mind made of the experience almost an extra-mural research project in Irish music. A look at the list of the players he used on his various programmes gives an indication of the importance he attached to examining the genuine tradition.

The singers included such notable names as Darach Ó Cathain, Seán Jack 'ac Dhonncha, Nioclas Tóibín, Seán de hÓra, Pádraig Ó Tuama and Máire Ní Cheocháin. Significantly, the last two were from Cúil Aodha, where Seán and his family were destined to live some years later.

Pipers included Tommy Reck from Dublin, the famous Johnny Doran, the travelling piper who had died in an accident a few years earlier, but who had, fortunately, been recorded by the Folklore Commission and Séamus Ennis, considered by many to be the best piper of his day. Fiddlers on Seán's list included John Doherty, John Gallagher and Vincent Campbell from Donegal, John Henry and Fred Finn from Sligo, John Kelly, Junior Crehan and Patrick Kelly from Clare. He used Patrick Ahearn to illustrate the west Limerick/north Kerry style.

Seán used part of his fiddle programme on the *Our Musical Heritage* series to launch an attack on the use of the piano to accompany traditional fiddle players. He couched it in typically forthright and uncompromising Ó Riada language:

> The use of the piano to accompany traditional fiddle-playing is unfortunately prevalent. This is a scar, a blight, on the face of Irish music and displays ignorance on the part of those who allow or encourage it. The reason for it is easy to see. It is a truism to say that we suffer in this country from a national inferiority complex. To combat it we have developed a number of tricks which we hope will fool others into thinking we are better than we are – while we are fooling only ourselves. The piano is such a 'trick'. It has become a symbol of respectability. The house that has a piano

looks down on the house that hasn't, even if the piano is never played ... The traditional fiddle-player who insists on a piano accompaniment is falling into the same trap of 'respectability' ... Irish traditional music well played on the fiddle is sufficient unto itself; a piano accompaniment, even the best possible, and harmonically correct, detracts from and confuses it. All the finesse of the fiddle player, all the subtlety, delicate touches and fine points are clouded over and coarsened. When a traditional player has a piano accompaniment, it is often not only not harmonically correct, it is a travesty ...

In discussing the flute, Seán pointed out that the instrument used by traditional players is the old wooden flute that preceded the modern metal instrument used by orchestral players. Though the wooden flute has a range of just two octaves, as opposed to the three octaves of the orchestral instrument, this is quite adequate for traditional music and its more mellow, warmer tone is better suited to Irish music.

In selecting players to illustrate his flute programme, Seán concentrated on performers from Sligo, Clare and west Limerick. Peter Horan, Mick Joe Ryan and Séamus Tansey are the Sligo performers, while Michael Tubridy (who played with Seán in Ceoltóirí Cualann), Michael Falsey and Peter O'Loughlin illustrate the rolling, ornamented style of Clare. John Joe Hartnett plays in the fast, rhythmical simpler style of west Limerick.

In Seán's programme on tin-whistle, Paddy Moloney illustrates the technique a piper brings to the whistle and, in fact, Ó Riada uses pipers almost exclusively to make his various points about whistle playing. The only whistler he uses, who is not a piper, is Seán Potts who, as Ó Riada explains, has piping in his blood! The other players are Willie Clancy and J.C. Talty, both Clare pipers.

In his *Our Musical Heritage* programmes, Ó Riada made it abundantly clear that he was not a fan of accordions, nor of accordionists.

Most accordion players are so hampered by their choice of instrument as to be unable to produce anything but a faint wheezy imitation of Irish music. And unfortunately this instrument, designed by foreigners for the use of peasants with neither the time, inclination nor application for a worthier instrument is gaining vast popularity throughout the country. The reason for this is mainly, I think, the laziness which afflicts us as a nation at the moment. We would all like to be musicians, but we don't want to take the trouble. It is easier to play notes ready-made for us than to make our own, so we turn to accordions – bigger and better accordions – eventually to the greatest abomination of all, the piano accordion. nothing could be further from the spirit of Irish music ...

About the average céilí band, playing Irish music, Seán has this to say:

The most important principles of traditional music – the whole idea of variation, the whole idea of the personal utterance – are abandoned. Instead, everyone takes hold of a tune and belts away at it without stopping. The result is a rhythmic but meaningless noise with as much relation to music as the buzzing of a bluebottle in an upturned jamjar.

However, it was not all negative: Ó Riada devoted some time to postulating the type of band he would recommend for public performance of Irish music. He saw group playing as an important way in which Irish music could develop. He postulated that there must be variety in the performance itself – he saw this variety, expressed through variation in the performance of particular pieces as being:

A keystone of traditional music ... It must not, therefore, flog away all the time, with all the instruments going at once, like present-day céilí bands. Ideally, it would begin by stating the basic skeleton of the tune to be played; this would then be ornamented and varied by solo instruments, or by small groups of solo instruments. The more variation the better, so long as it has its roots in the tradition, and serves to extend that tradition rather than destroy it by running counter to it.

As to the instrumentation of this imaginary ideal band: I think that all the instruments most suited for playing should be represented. The uilleann pipes, the flute and the whistle would make up a reasonable wind section. Fiddles there should be, of course, and also accordions to help fill out the passages where the whole band is playing. As for drums, the modern notion of using a jazz drum-kit is entirely out of tune with Irish music. Their sound is coarse and without subtlety. But I think that our native drum, the bodhrán, whose history goes back well into pre-Christian times, would be very suitable.

To provide variety with the bodhrán (since variation is the keynote) the bones are available ... I think also that a harp played in the traditional fashion would lend an edge, and occasional touches of harmony, to this ideal band.

It is clear that this was Seán's plan for Ceoltóirí Cualann. He did not have a harp for that band, but made up for the deficiency by his own use of the harpsichord, when he ceased playing bodhrán with the group. It is significant that the professional group which eventually grew from Seán's original band included a harp in their line-up. I refer of course to The Chieftains, under the leadership of Paddy Moloney.

It is difficult to balance Seán's recommendation of the harp with what he said about it around the same time in one of his *Irish Times* article:

The harp is a cursed bloody instrument. For one thing, it is always going out of tune, a source of much annoyance to me in the last few weeks, during which I've been experimenting with the instrument, in the hope of writing something for it.

Seán made hundreds of arrangements for Ceoltóirí Cualann for radio and television programmes. They were not musical arrangements in the normal sense of music written for each instrument, but instructions as to what tune should be played by what instrument or group of instruments.

Seán exerted more control over the music when they played O'Carolan pieces, with a greater involvement by him on harpsichord. Even though traditional musicians in those days did have a few O'Carolan pieces in their repertoire, it was Ó Riada who restored the music of the blind harper to the standard repertoire, with such pieces on record as *Pléaraca na Ruarcach*, with an attempt by Ó Riada to produce a rather ancient atmosphere, using only standard traditional instruments and harpsichord. Due to his influence, most Irish traditional music groups would now include *O'Carolan's Concerto*, *Morgan McGann*, *Fanny Power*, *O'Carolan's Farewell*, *Planxty Hewlett*, *Lord Inchiquin* and *Henry MacDermott Roe*.

Seán Ó Riada moved close to modern 'pop' with the famous Gael Linn recording of *An Poc ar Buile*, sung by Seán Ó Sé and accompanied by Ceoltóirí Cualann. The song, composed by Dónal Ó Mulláin, was immensely popular on Irish radio in the early 1960s. The brightness of Seán Ó Sé's fine tenor voice was a perfect foil for the musicians.

About the same time, Ó Riada made a setting for Pilib Ó Laoire's *Cór Cois Laoi* of six old Irish texts, entitled *Ceathrúintí Éagsúla*, which the choir sang at the Cork Choral Festival. It seems that Seán brought an atmosphere of seán-nós into at least one of the pieces, *Rop Tú mo Bhaile* and some of the writing presages what he was to produce later in his first mass for Cór Chúil Aodha.

Seán Ó Riada revolutionised the presentation of Irish music, and changed our attitudes and enriched our appreciation of what is fundamental to it.

CHAPTER 10

SEÁN Ó SÉ AND Ó RIADA

Seán Ó Sé had a very important place in the part of Ó Riada's life
that concerned bringing Irish music to the notice of the public in,
as it were, a new dress. But Seán Ó Sé was not an original member of
Ceoltóirí Cualann, though many think he was. The two Seán's came
from the very same background – something that Ó Riada understood
very well.

During one of their early recordings in Dublin, Ó Sé's first time
recording with full orchestra, he was, of course, very nervous. At one
of the intervals, Ó Riada bent down from the podium, where he was
conducting *Rhapsody of a River,* and said to the young singer, to
encourage him, 'don't mind that lot, son, but just remember that your
grandfather and mine stood side by side at the fair of Ballyvourney,
selling bonavs!'

Seán Ó Sé was singing with the Gael Linn cabaret when he first
heard Ceoltóirí Cualann on a radio programme called *Reacaireacht an
Riadaigh.* He remembers it was his mother who recommended he
should listen to them. 'They are a little bit mad,' she said to him, 'but
I love their music.' What most impressed Seán about them on a first
hearing was the singing of Darach Ó Cathain, particularly in the song

Peigín Leitir Mhóir. Hearing their first record, *Reacaireacht an Riadaigh,* Seán was very impressed with Ó Riada's arrangement of *Spailpín a Rúin,* especially in the second verse, when Éamonn de Buitléar joined in with accordion bass. Seán felt then he was getting a whole new view of the music.

It was intended that Seán Ó Sé should make a record for Gael Linn and he had already sent a sample tape to Dublin, through Diarmuid Ó Broin, who was manager of the Cabaret. *An Poc ar Buile* was the name of the song he chose, with harp accompaniment by Deirdre Ní Fhloinn, who was playing with the Cabaret at that time. The tape was given to Riobárd Mac Góráin and soon afterwards, to Seán Ó Riada. Subsequently, the singer received an invitation from Riobárd to go to Dublin to meet Seán Ó Riada in Riobárd's house. On meeting Ó Riada, Seán Ó Sé felt quite nervous, as the great musician was dressed in very arty clothes, with a briefcase under his arm and looking upper-class – or at least that was how he seemed to Seán. Riobárd introduced Ó Riada, to whom he gave a glass of whiskey, and it was not long before the audition began, for that is what it really was.

As soon as Riobárd left the room, the atmosphere changed and the singer felt that Ó Riada was more sympathetic towards him. Ó Sé thought that it might have something to do with their similar background in Cork. He sang the song, *An Clár Bog Déil,* accompanied by Ó Riada. It was the Seán Óg Ó Tuama version that he sang, just as he had learned it from the little book, *Claisceadal an Raidió.*

Seán was singing, at the top of his voice, the words which meant: 'I would marry you without cattle, without money, without any dowry, with the permission of your people,' when Ó Riada stopped him suddenly. 'In the name of Jesus Christ', said Ó Riada angrily, 'what credit would he get for marrying with her parents' permission? Without it, I tell you, without their blessing.' Then he said a few words, which were not very nice, about Seán Óg Ó Tuama and his habit of changing songs for the sake of religious purity, something which Ó Riada did not like, though it was common among collectors at that time.

They went through a few more songs and Ó Riada decided, on the spur of the moment, that they should go that evening to Peter Hunt's studio, where they recorded three songs: *An Buachaill Caol Dubh, Bean Dubh a' Ghleanna* and *An Poc ar Buile.*

Seán sang regularly on Fleadh Cheoil an Raidió from then on. He enjoyed the experience of appearing on the same programme as sean-chaí Éamonn Kelly and singer Seán Ó Síocháin: it was all so different from what he had been doing with the Blarney ceilí band and Cabaret Gael Linn. The recordings were made at first in St Francis Xavier Hall and later in the GPO Henry Street. One of the most popular songs with the studio audience was *Níl sé ina Lá,* arranged by Ó Riada so that, in the middle of the song, when they changed key from D to G, Seán Ó Síocháin's baritone voice could be heard an octave below the tenor.

The first time Seán Ó Sé sang in a public concert to Ó Riada's accompaniment was at a Comhchaidreamh concert in Foxhall Hotel in Raheny, in company with Barney McKenna and Seán McGuire. Ó Sé remembers two things from that night: firstly, that he sang *Cath Chéim an Fhia* and secondly, as he sang, he realised for the first time that he had never before encountered such a competent and sympathetic accompanist as Ó Riada. He still thinks of that moment as one of the most significant in his life, as he had never met an accompanist who could inspire one to such previously unexperienced heights of performance. He always felt that Ó Riada had almost magical power in his accompaniment – as if he could correct you in the very instant before you would make a mistake in the music!

Ó Sé remembers Ó Riada wearing cowboy boots that night, as he played and presented the concert: he still has an image of Ó Riada parading in all directions on stage, so that everyone in the audience could see his fancy attire. That was the first time Seán Ó Sé got an invitation to stay overnight in Galloping Green. 'I thought I'd never see another poor day', he has since commented.

Seán remembers that Rachel was turned out of her bed to make place for him. He slept late in the morning, until all the young Ó Riada's brought various parts of his breakfast to him in bed – Peadar, Rachel, Eoin and Alastair. Ruth was pregnant with Cathal at the time. Seán was impressed by the quiet good manners of the young Ó Riada family: it was only later he found out that Ó Riada was a firm believer in strict parental authority – especially that of the father!

Ó Riada took Seán into Dublin that morning in his Jaguar, JZE666. It was then that Ó Sé discovered how poor his famous friend really was. Ó Riada was expecting a cheque to come in the post that day and without it, he was only able to buy a single gallon of petrol at the pumps – scarcely enough, to bring them to the next petrol station. But the appearance of wealth did seem to matter to Ó Riada.

On another occasion they were to play at a concert in Kilrush, in County Clare. It was during the period when the family lived in Kerry and they were to meet at Benner's hotel in Dingle at lunchtime. Ó Sé was a few hours late in arriving and, at first could not find the Ó Riadas. The hotel porter was not able to help, but he glanced into the deserted restaurant, where he saw Ruth, with the child at her breast and Ó Riada beside her, laid back in the seat, puffing a cigar and surrounded by smoke. 'Christ,' said Ó Riada, 'I thought you'd never come. I can't leave this place, as I haven't a sou to pay for all this.' He stretched out his hands to indicate the empty plates. Seán Ó Sé paid the bill and they left for Kilrush. But Seán was keen to report that Ó Riada returned the money, as well as all other money he gave him on loan.

Seán remembers another incident on their return from Kilrush that evening. As there was no ferry, it was necessary to come to Limerick first and then west towards Dunquin. They visited a pub for a drink and while they were there the baby, Cathal, began to cry. Ó

Riada told Ruth to give him a 'dart' of the breast as they sat at the counter – which she did. Two old men seated beside them at the bar almost had a seizure when they saw Ruth breastfeeding the child in public, as it was not a common sight in County Clare in the early 1960s!

After Ó Riada came to Cúil Aodha in 1963, Seán Ó Sé and he would travel to Dublin monthly, to make radio programmes. On the Tuesday evening before the recording they used to practice in Ó Riada's little studio, beside his house. The singer would sometimes get tapes of the songs by post from Cúil Aodha, so that he could learn them at home. Ó Sé is still annoyed that he used the same tape, rather than giving Ó Riada a new one each time. What a unique collection of songs he would have had now – all sung by Ó Riada!

Ó Sé remembers another time when Ó Riada asked him to bring his mother, Julia Creedon, to a session they were to have in the basement of his house in Galloping Green. Ó Riada always liked, where possible, to have his father and mother at the the big events of his life. Seán's father did not often go, as his health was not good, but the mother always wanted to attend.

At other times, when Seán was going out to Cúil Aodha to practise for a recording, he would bring with him Ó Riada's parents, who lived in Cork city. Ó Riada had a strict rule that no one could come into the studio while they were practising, but often before the end of the session Ó Riada would indicate to Seán that they should practise a particular song with piano. That meant they had to go into the sitting room where, of course, the parents would be listening. Seán Ó Sé had no doubt that Ó Riada did this on purpose, for his parents' benefit.

Frequently, on the way home to Cork in the car, Julia would ask Seán to sing one of the songs they had been practising in Cúil Aodha. She might interrupt his singing to say: 'now, the lad (by which she meant her son) had a nicer turn there: you haven't got it right yet.' She always said Ó Riada had a special touch on the piano that she would recognise anywhere: both parents were extremely proud of their son.

Music for the sound-track of the film *Kennedy's Ireland* was the second symphonic piece in which Seán Ó Sé was involved with Ó Riada. Charles Davis, an Irishman living in America, was responsible for the organisation of the project. There were various songs to be sung, including *Boolavogue, Kelly the Boy from Killane* and a couple of emigration songs. Seán was with Ó Riada in Cúil Aodha the night before the Dublin recording, viewing parts of the film, when Ó Riada decided that the whole thing was too stage-Irish and he would have to change the theme music.

The two of them went to the post office in Cúil Aodha to telephone Davis about the matter. Ó Riada was very satisfied with himself, as he walked in and addressed Dónal Ó Liatháin: 'Dónal, my boy, could you get us Palm Springs 237468231?' Dónal showed no surprise at Ó Riada's request for such an exotic number and coolly asked Macroom for Palm Springs (this was in the days before the automatic exchange had reached the area).

Ó Riada spent a long time in conversation with Davis and Seán heard *The Shores of Amerikay* mentioned often. It was decided on the phone that it should be the new theme song for the film. Everything seemed well settled until they got back into the car. 'Christ in heaven,' Ó Riada shouted, 'how does that bloody song go?' They were in a fix now, having given up a song they knew for one they did not – and the following day was the deadline for recording it with orchestra in Dublin.

Seán Ó Sé told Ó Riada he thought Mike Murphy from Blackstone Bridge, near Cork, would know it. He was the father of Johnny Murphy who played with Ó Sé in the Blarney ceilí band. Seán jumped into his car and drove at speed, to Blackstone Bridge, where the father sang a verse into Seán's tape. It was the first verse – and the only one he had, but they eventually located the rest in an old edition of *Ireland's Own*, that was lying upstairs.

Back to Cúil Aodha where, at a very late hour, Ó Riada, having decided that the song would be in F, explained to Seán how he wanted it sung. Seán's Morris Minor was full of the strains of *The Shores of Amerikay* all the way back to his house in Cork. The following day, Seán went to Dublin and, on entering the Phoenix Hall, where the recording was to be made, was surprised to hear the orchestra practising their parts. It was clear that Ó Riada had spent the night in Cúil Aodha, writing out the parts, before taking the early train to Dublin.

However, within a short time, the project fell through when Kennedy was assassinated in Dallas. Thus ended another of Ó Riada's dreams of real wealth. The film was later shown at the Cork Film Festival but, for all practical purposes, Kennedy's death had killed the picture.

Ó Riada had many other such dreams: some of his wild schemes were intended to benefit himself, while others were meant to advance the prosperity of Cúil Aodha.

Seán Ó Sé remembered Ó Riada going to Canada in 1971 at the invitation of Professor Bob O'Driscoll for a conference to mark the dual centenary of Jack B. Yeats and John Millington Synge. Treasa O'Driscoll has described the event in her book I*n the Deep Heart's Core,* where she says: 'Seán's eagerness in accepting this invitation appeared to override his reluctance to "cross the Atlantic in an aeroplane" and his amusement at the smallness of the fee being offered to all participants: "I wouldn't blow my nose for $150 but I will come anyway!"' He eventually travelled to Toronto in the company of Anne Yeats.

Ó Riada planned, at one stage, to build a large hotel on the banks of the Sullane River, with an airport beside it, near where Peadar Ó Riada, some years ago, put on a river-pageant in honour of his father. Seán Ó Riada had intended to bring hundreds of visitors into the district to hunt and fish – and maybe even listen to music played by himself!

CHAPTER 11

Ó Riada as Writer

Apart from his obvious musical talent, Seán had considerable literary gifts. Even at school in Farranferris, he and fellow-student
Greehy were both far ahead of their class in their familiarity with the
classics of English as well as of Greek and Roman literature.

An examination of Seán's final year project for his B. Mus. degree
was made and apart from his musical maturity in analysing a very
modern piece of music by Schoenberg, his writing in this project on
Schoenberg's method of twelve-tone composition was quite impressive. He shows an independence of spirit that would later be obvious
in the more mature Ó Riada.

In this thesis, Seán analysed in detail Schoenberg's composition,
No. 5 of the Funf Klavierstucke, opus 23. Commenting on one aspect of
the work, Ó Riada writes: 'The music itself only manages to avoid
complete meaninglessness by the attempt at ternary form in which it is
written. One can almost hear Schoenberg's imagination creaking!'

Clearly, the young music student was not overawed by the avant
garde composer's new music:

... what does the average listener hear? A concatenation of sounds which are to him meaningless, deliberately discordant, devoid of even accidental concord. Without the average listener's attention, the Schoenbergian composer is left in his ivory tower, free to reproduce himself in his music in narcissistic fascination; this self-contemplation may be very pleasurable to himself but does not contribute one whit to the development of music.

It is a fact that Ó Riada in later life had recourse to twelve-tone composition in some of his major works. However, his use of it was always governed by his own genius and his work was closer to Berg, a disciple of Schoenberg. He was already indicating this in 1952, in this project, where he says:

> ... the music of Alban Berg, a follower of Schoenberg, as exempli-fied in his opera *Wozzeck*, sounds largely tonal. His treatment of the 'basic set' is not rigid, but flexible and he adapts "the basic set" to whatever the situation demands. This relaxation of the strict rules laid down by Schoenberg would seem to indicate a trend back to tonality, however vague and nebulous though it be at pre-sent. Berg's music is also noticeable for the smoothness and fluid-ity of its line – a virtue noticeable in Schoenberg's music by its absence.

The final paragraph shows something of Seán's breadth of knowl-edge, even as an undergraduate. It is, for me, a kind of Credo of the future composer's attitude to his art and his appreciation of art in gen-eral. He begins with a dismissal of strict twelve-tone composition:

> The Schoenberg method, as he himself has formulated it, cannot survive. Over-complexity is the rope with which it strangles itself. What is needed in music today is a return to simplicity and inno-cence. By this I mean that composers in the time to come must

learn to look at music from a fresh viewpoint, to see it, as it were for the first time.

In this respect, painting is far in advance of music. Composers must look at music as Picasso and Paul Klee looked at painting. Music is primarily an entertainment and an art. The search for beauty must be re-instituted through simplicity. Humility in approach is necessary. Catch phrases such as 'Art for Art's sake', 'Art for the sake of self-expression', etc. must be discarded.

The medieval spirit in art must be re-born. Music would be in a far better condition today if composers and the interpreters of their music were forced to remain anonymous, as the monks in the monasteries in the middle ages. Satie showed the road of return for music more than thirty years ago. This is the road which music must travel, if it is to continue being art for the people.

I found it surprising that Seán signed his name at the end of this project in both Irish and English. Before reading this document, it appeared that he first used the name Seán Ó Riada in the late 1950s, but he signed it in this way, in brackets, after John Reidy, in 1952.

In his later period as Musical Director at the Abbey Theatre, Seán was acknowledged in some of the programmes as writer of lyrics and composer of music, both for plays and for the annual Christmas pantomime in Irish, *Geamaireacht na Nollag*, where he co-operated with Tomás MacAnna, who highly valued Seán's writing skills.

Professor John A. Murphy of UCC remembers a projected play for television by Ó Riada, concerning which the two men had many discussions. It was to be called *Ireland at War* and Ó Riada wrote a script called *The Irish Soldiers* which is obviously a draft of the play. It has precise camera directions and music cues, even naming one singer, Nioclas Tóibín and songs and airs such as *Marbhna Luimní, Clare's Dragoons, Mo Ghile Mear, a Shaighdiúirín a chroí*. It would appear to be a quick-moving cameo of Irish involvement in war in Ireland,

Spain, France and in the American Civil War. Seán sought advice from Professor Murphy on many historical aspects of the various wars referred to in the script.

Seán published some poetry in Irish in the 1960s and wrote articles for the Irish magazine *Comhar*. His published poem, *An Feall* (deceit, treachery), is typical Ó Riada's delight in word-play:

AN FEALL
'Filleann an feall ar an bhfeallaire' –
Acht má 'sé an feallaire an file
An bhfillfidh an feall ar an bhfile?

As buile na feola 's na fola
Sea gheintear an file, instealladh
Filíochta; duine go h-uile
'Na fhile go mealladh.

Má's duine an file, má's file
An duine a geineadh mar gach uile
Breallaire: cá bhfuil an feallaire?
Ar an nduine a fhilleann an feall.

TRANSLATION:
The wrong returns to the wrongdoer
But if he be a poet, tell me
What then? what then?
Will the wrong return to the rhymer?

A poet is born of the madness
The Muse injects in flesh and blood
Bemusing him, confusing him,
Transfusing person into poetry.

If poet then be person
Like all us human fools
What then? what then?
The *feall* returns to the fool.

An earlier poem he wrote for the annual Court of Poetry –
Dámhscoil Mhúscraí, in Cúil Aodha, January 1964, answered the poetic question on the new Irish television service, Telefís Éireann, posed
for the gathering of poets. It was subsequently published in *Comhar*.
Seán specified the traditional air to which it was to be sung.

THE IRISH TIMES ARTICLES BY Ó RIADA

When Seán went to live in Kerry towards the end of 1962, after leaving the Abbey Theatre, he wrote a series of articles for *The Irish Times*.
These were to be an important source of income for him for the next
eight months, before his appointment to the Music Department of
University College Cork. He was, of course, working independently
for Irish radio, both with *Reacaireacht an Riadaigh* programmes and
with his important *Our Musical Heritage* series.

1. 13 NOVEMBER 1962:

FOX AND HOUNDS BY SEÁN Ó RIADA

An echoing 'Tally-ho' through the clear, cold air of a November morning trumpets the beginning of the hunting season. What was it that
Oscar Wilde called foxhunting? – 'The pursuit of the uneatable by the
unspeakable,' a typical jackeen's wisecrack. Had Oscar been a poultry
farmer (rather nice idea – deep litter or battery system?) instead of a
salon wit, he mightn't have been so quick to defend the hunted against
the hunter.

'Morrow, Fox.'
'Morrow Sir.'

SEÁN Ó RIADA

OUR MUSICAL HERITAGE

Edited by Thomas Kinsella
Music Editor: Tomás Ó Canainn

FUNDÚIREACHT AN RIADAIGH
i gcomhar le
THE DOLMEN PRESS

Publication in 1982 of Seán
Ó Riada's seminal analysis of
the state of Irish traditional
music.

'What is that you're eating?'
'A fine fat goose I stole from you,
And when will you come and taste it?'

Ancient sport

Since the earliest times, according to the old manuscripts, hunting was
the chief sport of the old Gaelic nobility. It is recorded that that leg-
endary character, Fionn Mac Cumhaill, devoted six months of the year
to it. In those days, of course, they hunted the stag, the wild boar, and
the wolf. But wolves and wild boars disappeared from our landscape
many centuries ago (although cultivation of domesticated swine is an
important feature of contemporary Ireland) and by the middle of the
seventeenth century stag hunting was already a thing of the past, as we
can see from the greatest of the Gaelic hunting songs of that period
(George Sigerson's translation):

It is my sorrow sorest,
Woe – the falling forest!
The north wind gives me no rest,
And death's in the sky.
My faithful hound's tied tightly,
Never sporting brightly,
Who'd make a child laugh lightly
With tears in his eye.
The antlered noble-hearted
Stags are never started,
Never chased nor parted
From the furzy hills ...

That song in Gaelic *Seán O Duibhir a Ghleanna*, is attributed to
one John O'Dwyer, of Cloniharp Castle in County Tipperary. He
fought beside his cousin Colonel Edmund O'Dwyer in the anti-

Cromwellian war of 1649-1652. The colonel surrendered in March 1652, a conditional surrender, and was allowed to take his army of 4,500 officers and men to Flanders, where they joined the Spanish army under the Prince of Condé. It is highly probable that John O'Dwyer of the song, his cousin, went with him. Thus did the old Gaelic nobility give place to the foreign upstart, the Cromwellian gombeen-man. Thus did the hunters become the hunted.

The boar hunt, the wolf hunt, the stag hunt – all gone, all finished, 'with O'Leary in the grave'. All that remains is foxhunting. On the whole, I think it is a good thing that it remains, even though a fair percentage of our metropolitan hunters (riding hired horses and wearing borrowed clothing) wouldn't know a fox from a foxhound, a brush from a broom. These are the people who usually end up in the heel of the hunt, who live in mortal terror of a stone wall, who think hunting would be 'jolly good fun' (phoney English accent) if only the fox were not involved.

The farmer who has a Hunt Club in his vicinity is a lucky man. Even if he does not participate in its activities, he is entitled to compensation for any of his fowl killed by a fox. Similarly, he has his duty to the Hunt, to inform them if he knows of a fox in the neighbourhood. In this way both sport and domestic economy are served. Can the same be said of golf? Or table tennis?

I suppose the greatest hunt of all time is the one described in the nineteenth-century Gaelic song *Fiach an Mhadaruaidh*. The hunt began somewhere in north-west Cork, near where the new television transmitter will be, on Mullaghanish (I wonder was it the beginning of the Duhallow Hunt?). The song enumerates the principal riders – the Powers of Cappoquin, Arthur Russell of Banteer, the Whites of Bantry, Rhody Arthur (with his Lang-go-lee), Woulfe, Rattler, Hedges and Grainger from Macroom, and Captain Bull. The fox first headed for Limerick, but changed his mind near the county border and headed east towards Waterford. Down he came by Cappoquin, through the main street of Lismore, and west again, until he was 'found' in the end, up in the Sliabh Luachra mountains. It sounds like a week's hard riding to me, but even if it never happened, it makes a good story, especially when it's sung.

Epic hunts

That hunt, however, was nothing compared to the hunt that the poet Diarmuid Na Bolgaighe (Poxy Dermot) had in mind. Born just about 200 years ago, he lived to see great poverty towards the end of his life. One day he called into this old woman living near Glengarriff and begged her for sustenance of one kind or another. And if he did, he got, as they say, 'the dirt', when she turned him out of the house with a few well-chosen words. Smarting from the insult, Diarmuid wrote a poem, a satire, in which he described what he would do to her:

> I'll arise nice and bright in the morning,
> And whistle up my fine pack of hounds
> And we'll search through the hills and the valleys,
> Till we hunt her right into the ground –
> And it's Tally! hi ho! hi ho!
> Tally! hi ho! the wretched one!
> Tally! hi ho! she's found!
> The terrible hag of misery!

Ah, isn't it a fine thing on a clear, frosty morning to be trotting over the frozen stubble, with breath making smoke-rings on the crystal air, the sudden darting flight of a snipe, and then, echoing and re-echoing over the baying of hounds, the magical 'Gone away! Go-o-one away'.

2. TUESDAY 20 NOVEMBER 1962:
OUTCASTS OF THE ISLAND BY SEÁN Ó RIADA
The last time I was on the Great Blasket island, two or three years ago,

the island's population consisted of a few sheep, several thousand rabbits, and one solitary hen. This poor lonely creature has now been joined by some rich American ladies, ready, willing, and eager to share her exile. It is a pity that they are rich Bostonians, and not liberals from Rhode Island (the hen, too, is a Rhode Island Red, poultry farmers please note). I gather that it is their intention to make of the island a haven of *luxe calme et volupté*, something which generations of islanders could not succeed in doing. But when the bad weather comes, and the *dubhluachair* raises black, 100-foot-high waves, marooning them on their island, let them remember the angry shades of Muiris Ó Súilleabháin (who wrote *Twenty Years A-Growing*), Peig Sayers (who wrote *Peig*), and Tomás Ó Criomhthain (*An t-Oileánach*), who wrote prophetically at the end of his book, *ni bheidh ár leithéidí arís ann* – 'our likes will not be there again'. It was true for Tomás Ó Criomhthain: his likes will not be there again. Instead, the Great Blasket has become a suburb of Boston, Mass.

***

Where, in the name of God, is all this nonsense going to stop? Every day we are busily exporting Irishmen, and every day we are busily importing foreigners. If this continues, the day will surely come when Irishmen will be a minority in their own country, as they are in every other country. And then, perhaps, it will be the concentration camp for us as it was for the Jews (some of our importees have a certain understanding of that trade.) Our biggest export, whether by value, by weight, or by numbers, is the export of our own people. Thus we are continuing and developing a policy inaugurated by the British during the Famine years. (Those were the days before John Bull, arrogant, powerful, imperious, became John Bullock, baffled, impotent, waiting for the humane killer). An eighteenth-century quatrain runs:

101

Do threasgair an saol is shéid an ghaoth mar smál
Alastram, Saeusar, 'san mhéid sin 'bhí 'na bpáirt:
Tá an Teamhair 'na féar, is féach an Traoi mar atá.
Is na Sasanaig féin, b'fhéidir go bhfaghhaidis bás.

Time has banished like dust blown on the wind
Caesar, Alexander, and all their kind:
Troy is destroyed, Tara's grass and heath –
The English too, in their time, must suffer death.

This is no country for young men – unless they are politicians, or foreigners, or have inherited money. It seems to be a law of present-day Ireland that if a farmer with less than fifty acres has three sons, all three will emigrate. This is especially true if they are native speakers of Irish. Of the population of the Blasket Islands, less than a quarter are now living on the mainland; the remainder have left the country which refused to support them, or their language, or their traditions. The country that was won by such costly sacrifice, that was bought with the blood of good men, is being sold, physically, spiritually with its people, by its people, for the customary thirty pieces of electro-plated nickel silver. This is more than a scandal, more than a disgrace. It is the betrayal of every man who through the centuries took up arms for this country's freedom. Freedom for what? Freedom to emigrate.

***

However, let us leave that aside for the time being, and let us instead return to the Great Blasket with its lonely hen. Hens are by nature gregarious creatures; consider, then, the appalling depths of loneliness that this poor bird must have plumbed, isolated as she was amidst this sprawling, ever-increasing colony of rabbits. Would it not have been a wise, charitable and merciful gesture on the part of the Department of Agriculture to provide a small grant for the purchase of a cock, who would provide companionship and solace, and break the endless tedium of the waves, ceaselessly battering the island? It would also have been a profitable gesture, for the island is free of natural predators like rats and foxes, and in the fullness of time the colony of rabbits would be joined by a thriving colony of chickens.

***

Loneliness is not uncommon in the Blasket islands to-day. On one of the smaller islands, Beginish, there lives a jackass, who marooned himself there eight or nine years ago. A truly Joseph Conradian figure, he cannot but feel at times that his self-enforced isolation is wearing a bit thin. Sometimes at night, sleepers in Dunquin on the nearby mainland are awakened to hear him braying his sad song to the moon; visitors to the Great Island as they pass his little plot of rocks and moss, are occasionally startled by the sight of his ancient, hoary face peering at them from behind some outcropping. Here surely, is another cause that might, with enthusiasm, be taken up by some of our Nuclear Disarmers and 'Stoppers of the export of horses to Belgium'. I can see them now, an orderly dignified protest march, passing the Department of Agriculture offices with mournful and accusing look, bearing placards with signs such as 'Equal Rights for Jackasses', 'Save the Outcast of Beginish,' 'Beginish To-day – Ireland's Eye To-morrow?'

> *Mar a dubhairt an t-é 'dubhairt é:*
> *Ní hí an Eire-seo an Eire do bhí anallód ann*
> *Ach Éire lucht Béarla agus anstró Gall.*
> *Éire gan éifeacht 'sí i n'anró fann,*
> *Éire gan Ghaelig 'sis searbh leo rann.'*

Our Irish life and customs we've forsaken,
For English ways of speech and foreign parading,
A 'most distressful country' weak and ailing

To criticism Deaf, and Dumb to Gaelic.

3. SATURDAY 1 DECEMBER 1962
DEATH AND THE POET BY SEÁN Ó RIADA
'Cabhair ní ghoirfead go gcuirfear mé i gcruinn-chomhrainn' ('I'll not cry
'Help' before I'm narrow-coffined'), wrote the poet Aogán O Rathaille.
It was his last poem, a cry of defiance in the teeth of fate. It ends:

> I will stop henceforth, for death's dark shade is near,
> And dead are the dragon-proud princes of Léin and Lee;
> I shall follow those great-loved heroes who lately ceased –
> My fathers followed their fathers before Christ's deed.

This arrogant attitude to death was not common to all the Gaelic
poets of the eighteenth century; more often than not attitudes ranged
from resignation at the thought of man's ultimate fate, to horror before
the masked, hooded figure which was the medieval personification of
Death. Thus does Death speak, in an anonymous quatrain referring to
a skull:

> *Féach an ceann gan ann acht áit na súl,*
> *Féach an drandal mantach bearnach úd:*
> *A fhir úd thall, cé reamhar, cé áluinn thú.*
> *Beidh do cheann gan amhras ann mar siúd.*

> 'See the head with only holes for eyes,
> See the mumping mouth that soundless cries;
> My fair, fresh, fleshy, foolish, pretty boy,
> Your head one day will yellow hollow lie.'

And in another anonymous quatrain, Death speaks again in no
uncertain terms:

Tógaim an seán atá cráidhte liath, etc.

The white-haired senior and his wife I take;
The bright-beaked blackbird and his life I take:
The lively youngling and his fame I take:
All who live now and are to come, I take.

It is said of Eoghan Ruadh Ó Súilleabháin, reputedly the greatest sensualist of modern Gaelic literature, that his last words were addressed to a girl who was even then looking for his favours. Since the original Gaelic quatrain *Bean is trí fichid do chuireas fé'm lámhaibh amú* is unsuitable for publication in a family newspaper, I give here a translation which I have watered down considerably:

Of generous women I pleasured three score and three,
The finest in Munster I chose and they chose me;
Those days are ended, closed never more to be ...

Different Tone
On another occasion, however, when he was in the whole of his health Eoghan adopted a different tone of voice.

Dá bhfaghainn-se bás amáireach, d'fhágainn le hudhacht é, etc.:

If I should die to-morrow, don't put me in the graveyard.
But lay me in the alehouse, underneath the table.
Where the pints and quarts and bottles, and the tapping of the
    barrel
Would make far finer music than a swarm of bloody cuckoos –
And it's open up the porter, boys and fill my jug up full!

Despite his rakish character Eoghan Ruadh Ó Súilleabháin was without doubt the greatest lyric poet of the eighteenth century. His verse is characterised by its precise imagery, which is often concealed by a wealth of musical ornament. The form which he practised most consistently was the *Aisling* or vision-poem, in which the poet treats Ireland as if she were a woman.

One of the finest of his *Aisling*s is *im aonar seal* which I have taken the liberty of translating rather loosely, in order to preserve the original metre and rhyme scheme as far as possible. Here it is:

'Through banks of mist I walked alone
As night came on, so chill and vast.
When graceful as a sailing swan,
A maid as fair as dawn advanced.
Her walk was proud and stately,
Her eyes with liquid light did shine.
Her golden tresses, trailing,
Around my soul like serpents coiled.

'Oh, who are you sweet lady?
What fate escorts you through the night?
Are you Helen bright or Deirdre?
Or Venus born of form divine?'
In sorrow's tones she answered me,
'No goddess, but a maid alone
In bondage to adversity
And all my heroes dead and gone.'

Now sound the trumpet, beat the drum.
Now sharpen pike: unsheath the sword.
Now loudly let the roaring gun
Sing freedom's song abroad once more.

Let fire, and air and ocean
Resounding toll my lady's cause.
And blood flow darkly over
The petals of the secret rose.

Decadence

How weak, by comparison, this otherwise charming *Aisling* (anony-mous) from the late nineteenth century in the period of the language decadence: (Last night in my loneliness – *Aréir is me go huaigneach*)

As I lay down last evening, in sore distressful grieving.
The light of day was leaving and stars came in the sky,
When by my side appearing a maiden fair and queenly,
To me far sweeter-seeming than music was her sigh.
Her brow was wide and beaming, her eyes were brightly gleaming.
Her golden hair was teeming round her shoulders, white as snow.
Her gracious bosom heaving, her gaze so pure and seemly,
Her glance with love did pierce me and did me overthrow.

The influence of English ballads is obvious, and it was not long before they finally wiped out the traces of Eoghan Ruadh O Súilleabháin.

4. TUESDAY 4 DECEMBER 1962
LES NEIGES D'ANTAN BY SEÁN Ó RIADA
'Christmas is coming, the geese are getting fat
Please put a penny in the poor man's hat.'

I see where the shopkeepers have once more anticipated the anniversary of the birth of Christ by a month. The evening streets are glaring under their festoons of harsh lights, while in most of the larger stores the apprentices are fitting on the ritual moth-eaten false beards and red robes. And bearded men (or ladies) who show themselves abroad are followed by grinning youngsters shouting 'Lookit – Santy Claus!' Razors will be much in demand as Christmas presents.

And this brings us back to the shopkeepers. I find it rather odd, in bad taste, and I think, extremely immoral, that Our Lord's Coming should be used as an occasion to hoodwink people into buying more than they can afford, and a great deal of it useless rubbish, at that. However, perhaps I am being old-fashioned and reactionary. I find all these money-making devices which go under the general name of 'markets' somewhat suspicious: the Christmas 'market', which was invented about a hundred or so years ago; the teenage 'market' which was invented far more recently (when I was that age I was an adolescent – the English language, like Irish, has begun to decay): and of course we must not forget the so very Common Market. 'To market, to market, to buy a fat pig' – now, there's a really useful present.

The steamroller

The earliest Christmas I remember was when I was four years old, and saw something which was stamped incredibly clear on my memory ever since. It was a cold, frosty morning, and my parents had been to the six o'clock mass, but because of my tender age, I was allowed to stay in bed until the nine o'clock mass. As my mother and I walked home through the village, I saw for the very first time in my life, a steamroller.

It was parked just outside a public house, a fact which has occasioned me much bafflement whenever I think about it. How did a steamroller come to be parked outside a public house on the morning of Christmas Day?

Where was the driver – in the pub? At that hour of the morning? And if so, where did he come from? Surely, if he wanted to go to the pub, it would have been quicker for him to walk? Or maybe it was a stolen steamroller, abandoned outside the pub. But I hardly think so – a stolen steamroller is hardly the easiest thing in the world to get rid of, especially if it is such a conspicuous one as this one was, a great big black and gold monster. Before we went home we called to a neighbour's house to wish them a happy Christmas, and the woman of the house gave my mother and me a drop of port each to warm us, the only drink considered suitable in those days for women and children. Had the vision of the steamroller come after this, it would have been more easily explainable, but no, it came before. Another of life's unsolved mysteries.

A poet's apology

In the year 1729, the poet Diarmuid Mac Domhnaill Mac Finghin Chaoil Uí Shúilleabháin sent an apology to a friend because he could not be with him for Christmas. The reason, as he explains so eloquently in his verses *(An Braonda Shiar)*, was that he feared he would be made drink much by his hospitable host. Here is a somewhat rough, shortened translation:

> Old friend, dear old acquaintance, do not think me cool
> If I do not come to visit you: you know it's not my rule
> To stay away at Christmastime: 'tis just that, like a fool,
> I'm afraid of being bedevilled by the brandy bowl.

> It's an enemy of God and a destroyer of the soul:
> It thrusts the bravest bodies into the deepest hole,
> It surely came from Acheron or Styx so black and foul,
> That serpent-cunning, tricky, wicked brandy bowl.
> It isn't fear of travelling keeps me at home,
> Nor poverty, senility, nor anyone I mourn,
> Nor the journey over mountain-pass, not winter's icy cold –
> It's the thought of being confounded by the brandy bowl.

> The giddy child, or reckless, who falls into a hole,
> Or cuts himself, or burns his hand upon a fiery coal

Soon profits by the lessons learnt in such a bitter school –
Not otherwise have I been taught by countless brandy bowls.

I'd come – I'd be delighted to be sitting in your hall
But that your hospitality would tempt me to a fall
Accept my dearest wishes for yourself, your wife, and all,
From a sick, hungover fellow, bitten by a brandy bowl.

It is a curious thing (or is it?) that the poets of Ireland have always had what is called a 'weakness' for drink. One of them, an eighteenth-century poet called Seán Ó Tuama, kept a public house in Croom, County Limerick, where anyone who could compose a passable verse was allowed to drink on the house. His wife, who was a more thrifty character, however, took care that too much of the profit did not thus melt away, by watering or otherwise diluting such free drinks as were served.

A regular customer, another poet called Aindrias Mac Craith, complained vigorously about this in a satirical poem on Seán Ó Tuama. Ó Tuama replied with another satire, and the two poets continued to exchange verses which became gradually more and more libellous and obscene until they ended up in a silence of scurrility. And all because of drink. I'm sure the poets of Ireland will, this Christmas, as for centuries of Christmases, make sure that at least this Gaelic tradition is kept alive, be they Gaelic-speakers or English-speakers. Whiskey is a linguist.

Afterthought: I have just thought of what may be the possible solution of the steamroller mystery. Something like this: the driver, who had been drinking heavily on Christmas Eve, was ejected from his own pub when he got obstreperous. Since his legs could not be depended on to carry him, he looked about for the safest conveyance he could find, and obviously nothing could be better than a steamroller (whether it was his own or not doesn't matter). He managed to get to the pub where I saw it parked, and went in. After a few more drinks he

got more obstreperous, whereupon the publican sent for the guards. A
guard arrives, arrests him, charging him with being 'drunk in charge of
a steamroller', and puts him in the lock-up, where he was still sleeping
it off the following morning. Well, anyway, it could have happened
that way – or can anybody think of a better explanation?

(The newly-coined Irish for 'teenagers' is '*déagóirí*').

5. Saturday 15 December 1962
Grim Fairy Tales by Seán Ó Riada

In the days before such modern conveniences as radio, television and
the atomic bomb were visited upon us, country people had to depend
on their own resources for their entertainment. As soon as the long
winter nights came the visiting season was on, and they would call to
each other's house for a night's music, or card-playing or storytelling.
At home, the card games we usually played were forty-five, or hundred-and-ten (penny a round and tuppence a ring): nothing fancy like
bridge or Canasta, games which seem to me to be far too much like
work. (A friend of mine recently, on the occasion of a dispute, wrote
Hoyle, the card-games expert, for definite information regarding the
rules of hundred-and-ten. The answer he got was that Hoyle 'had no
information regarding this subject beyond that it was a game played by
swineherds in west Cork'. By damn, but I wouldn't mind having a few
swine to herd at that.)

Music was another matter demanding a little more formality.
Whereas card-playing was a group activity, with everyone taking part,
music was essentially a matter of individual performance, a solo effort.
The fiddle player, or flute player, or singer, while performing, was
apart from the group around the fire, who listened with a critical ear.
Their comments were usually candid but not often kind. 'Hang up
that fiddle, boy, before you cut your finger on it!' 'Did you see the beak
of him at the flute? – is it trying to whistle through it you are?' Or to
the female singer: 'Begod, Mary, I never thought you'd get through it

111

without getting your death from choking.' It was all very encouraging, I'm sure.

Apart from music and card-playing, as I said, the other main form of entertainment was storytelling. The stories would range from the simple re-telling of local events to the longer, almost 'classical' type of story about something in the past. One such story, which was my favourite, and often took a night in the telling was the one about the tinker and the cattle-jobber. Briefly this is what happened:

Some years ago, there was a street in the town of Macroom called Bothar na Sop or sop road (I think it's now known as New Street). and one evening towards nightfall, a cattle-jobber from Kenmare, went into a lodging house there. He was going to the fair in Millstreet the following morning and he left instructions with the yardboy to call him about an hour before dawn. Later on the same evening a tinker came to the same lodging-house. He had walked all the way from Killarney, and he was footsore and weary. They had no spare bed for him, so he had to share with the jobber and before he went upstairs he left instructions not to call him until the following evening, Well and good. The jobber was already asleep when the tinker arrived, but when he got into the bed the jobber woke up, and they spoke for a few minutes, each telling the other (whom he couldn't see in the darkness) of who he was, where he had been, where he was going, and when he was getting up. Then they went to sleep.

***

Now earlier on in the day, a doctor from the town had come to visit a sick man in the house next door to the lodging house. The patient had a fever of some kind, due, possibly, to a head injury, and the doctor said he would come back to shave his head, for, said he, 'It will cool him anyway, even if it does nothing else.' 'Now as the doctor was on his way to the sick man's house, he met a friend, and they had to have a drink. Then they had another, and one or two more after that. The result was that the doctor went to the wrong house in Bothar na Sop.

The two houses were built on the same plan, and the doctor, going up to the sick man's room, as he thought, arrived instead where the tinker and the jobber were asleep. The tinker was huddled beneath the clothes for warmth, but the jobber's head was outside. The doctor thereupon took out his razor and shaving-gear, and after he had got up a good lather on the jobber's head, he shaved him as bald as a duck-egg. 'There now,' he said to himself, 'that will keep him nice and cool until morning.' With that, he took himself off. On the way home, he met another friend, and again they lay into the drink. Suddenly the doctor thought, 'Heavens above, I left my instruments behind, and if that man cuts his throat by accident in the middle of the night, 'tis I'll be blamed.'

Off with him again to Bothar na Sop, and upstairs into the room. Now the tinker and the jobber had a fairly restless night, although they remained asleep, and the jobber was now down at the foot of the bed while the tinker had his head stuck out at the top. In came the doctor, a lamp in his hand, and when he saw the tinker, with his fine head of hair, his eyes nearly jumped out of his head. 'No wonder you had a fever, my poor man,' he thought. 'I shaved you only a couple of hours ago, and there's the hair after growing again. That growth would give anyone a headache. What will they say in Cork and Dublin when they hear about this? My name is made in medical history!

'How lucky I kept the first fleece in my bag as proof!' So saying, he shaved the tinker as bald as he had shaved the jobber. Then he went off, his heart singing.

***

It was well after dawn when the jobber was called in the morning. He looked out the window at the sun's rays and felt the anger rise in him. As he hurried to put on his clothes, he caught sight of the tinker's bald head, but he was too rushed to talk to him about it. He ran downstairs, and struck off out the road to Millstreet. It was a fine morning in early summer, and though it was very early, the sun's warmth and the heat of his running made him perspire. Added to this was the thought that if he didn't hurry, his journey would be wasted because all the beasts at the fair would have been sold. About four miles out the road, on the left-hand side, there is a well of clear spring water. He ran to it, to calm his thirst. When he looked down he saw the bald head staring back at him. Without pausing to think, he wheeled around and headed back for Macroom at a hand-gallop, nor did he stop until he arrived in the yard of the lodging house. He called the yardboy. 'Look here,' he said, 'this is a nice thing, and no doubt.' 'What thing?' said the yard boy. 'Weren't you told to call the jobber before dawn?' 'Well,' said the yard boy. 'I called him as early as I could.' 'If you did,' said the jobber, 'you called the wrong man!'

That's my story, and if there's a lie in it, 'tisn't my making.

6. WEDNESDAY 19 DECEMBER 1962
DEPRESSION OVER IRELAND
'An ghaoth aduaidh, bíonn sí cruaidh, is cuireann sí fuacht ar dhaoine.'

> The northern wind is harsh and wild and freezes all the people:
> The southern wind is soft and mild and nourishes well the
> seedlings:
> The western wind is good and kind, brings shoals of fish for eating:
> The eastern wind is sharp and dry and shivers the night with freezing.

It is said that the English, as a rule, devote more of their time to discussing the weather than anybody else – a complete fallacy. In this, as in so many other aspects of civilised life, they are merely trotting after us, so far behind as to be practically invisible. In the rural areas, especially, the technique of weather discussion has been raised to the level of a fine art.

Bad weather, naturally enough, is often associated or synonymous with bad luck for the farmer, and the signs of approaching storms are also frequently taken as signs of imminent misfortune. For the benefit of those *Irish Times* readers who are either meteorologists or fortune-tellers (they have, after all, a certain amount in common), here is a list of things to watch for:

Weather Signs

Signs of bad weather approaching: crows flying very low; the cows who were turned out to graze turning back into the yard; if a dog is sleeping by the fireside, that his stomach rumbles: the geese in the field suddenly taking a short flight: broken cloud fragments scudding across the sky (*madra gaoithe*): the cat sitting with its back to the fire; ducks shaking their wings as if about to fly; a sour taste in the mouth on awakening in the morning. (This last, however, may be merely a sign of personal heavy weather the previous night.)

The first time you hear the cuckoo in spring, if the call is on your left, it presages ill-luck for the year or bad weather for the year. (This last has been a pretty safe bet for the last few years). But of all the weather-predicting scenes, I suppose that the most well-known is the one about the distant hills seeming close being a sign of rain, or the same if they are shrouded in mist. (Digression: it is said that the three parts of magic are: mist, sailing and music).

I don't know if it's my imagination or not – in fact I'm certain it isn't – but for the last few years the weather seems to have completely lost its reason. We had no summer this year, only a mild winter. Now we're getting the hard winter, but even that is not consistent. A few cold days to get us muffled up, then a mild day to get us de-muffled and disarmed, and then an absolutely freezing day when we don't expect it distributes the common cold with a lavish and impartial hand.

Something should be done about it, but by whom? The Tourist

Board? Or the Government? Perhaps a special department could be set up to deal with the situation. If this country were a monarchy, the Minister in charge would have to be temporarily ennobled. 'At Question Time in the Dáil yesterday, Sir Hardy Frost, KBW (Knight of the Big Wind), Minister for Weather Control and Tourism, in reply to a question from Mr Padraig MacSneachta, T.D. (N.P.D.), said that the Rain-Distribution Commission (*Coisde na Báisti*) were considering ways and means of adding fluorine to certain selected showers …'

Blasket Memory

When the weather behaves in a particularly deranged fashion, there is sometimes consolation to be found in the thought that it is bound to be worse somewhere else. Tomás Ó Criomhthain, who wrote *An t-Oileánach* (The Islandman), kept a diary of his life on the Great Blasket Island, in which he describes some truly diabolical weather. Here, in translation, is an entry describing a comparatively mild day in the winter of 1920:

> It is a winter's day with all the signs of it. The force of the gale is blowing the sea up over the land wherever it is able to do so. There is no sight to be had of the wave peaks of the sea, because of the storm and the thick white foam that is covering them up. The grass that was green yesterday is rotted and withered today. The skin of the people themselves is changing with the bad weather. The sheep of the hill are blown away from their grazing-places, and they are trying to come into the houses to us. The fish that was all through the year basking on top of the water in the sunshine has been sent out of sight by the storm. The young woman that all through the year was as graceful and stately as the swan on the lake, when she comes in with the bucket of water, the comb that was on her head has been robbed from her by the wind, her hair is blowing into her mouth, her clothes are all muddied and bedraggled, half of the

bucket is spilt, and she is as depressed as somebody who would be in the want of tobacco. The elderly people whose bones were so soft and fine all during the year, with the heat of the sun, one of them has a leg giving way on him, another has a hand threatening him with trouble. Still another sitting in on top of the rim of the fire, with an eye being kept on him for fear he would fall into it with the sleep. There is a great cure in the good weather, but many evils follow the bad.

Far-off Sun

Summer seems very far off, now that the days are mostly night and the sun is hiding. However, I suppose it will come again, even if it only lasts for a day or two, and if the winter leaves any one of us alive to see it, something that seems doubtful at the moment. I don't know. Maybe the weather will improve? We're due for a change anyway. You'd never know, it might turn out mild. Anyway, it won't be as bad as we think, for, as the rhyming quatrain has it:

> *Dhá dtrian gaoithe ag crannaibh,*
> *Dhá dtrian sneachta ar shléibhtibh*
> *Dhá dtrian uisce ar mhóintibh,*
> *Is dhá dtrian córa ag fear céille.*

> Two-thirds of the wind are in the trees;
> Two-thirds of the snow on the mountains,
> The bogs get two-thirds of the water,
> And a man of sense is two-thirds in the right.

7. SATURDAY 29 DECEMBER 1962
THE MUSICAL LIFE AND COWS BY SEÁN Ó RIADA
The harp is a cursed bloody instrument. For one thing, it is always going out of tune, a source of much annoyance to me in the last few

repeat

weeks, during which I've been experimenting with the instrument in the hope of writing something for it. One would have thought that the traditional harpers, who used brass strings (which they played with curved fingernails – *aduncis unguibus*, as Stanihurst put it in 1584), would not have had to cope with this problem to the same extent. One would be wrong. The brass strings which they used seem to have gone out of tune nearly as quickly as the gut or nylon strings of today. Then, as now, this faulty intonation brought the harpers much carping and obloquy from the music critics of their time. Here is an example of such criticism from the pen of the seventeenth-century Kerry poet, Tadhg Ruadh Ó Conchubhair, appraising the ability of a harper called Eoin Óg Mac Gafraidh:

Eoin at sour notes is clever
But ignorant of proper play;
Like a sow's grunting lullaby
His clumsy, buzzing semiquavers.

His twitching shoulders mime the notes
His fumbling thumbs cannot bring out;
Like a mangy cur's hungry snout
His foolish hands snap at the chords.

Just as the tender sucking pig
When bitten by a puppy crass,
His silly fingers, plucking brass
Sing the same sad, complaining jig.

His diligence is wonderful
As he searches out a chord:
Strange, that such a small reward
Crowns these labours, pitiful.

Your tune, or mine, whenever it
Unlucky, haps under his thumb,
(What dismal, boring, stubborn hum!)
Porridge is what he makes of it.

Bitter 'tis, that sweet-voiced harp
Should be enslaved by such a fool:
No key, no string, no air, no rule,
That won't 'twixt these dumb fingers, warp.

***

So much for a bad harper! Those were really the palmy days of music criticism in Ireland. Perhaps some of our contemporary music critics might try to revive the style? It would, at the very least, make for lively reading, far livelier than some of the dreary music which it is sometimes their unhappy lot to have to criticise. Generally speaking our contemporary music critics are gentle, patient, softspoken people. They hesitate to brand as rubbish the compositions of scribblers who would be better, and more productively employed, cutting turf or thinning beet; they soothe with soft words those farm-labourers manqués (from whatever part of the world) who, on occasion display their conspicuous lack of virtuosity in musical performance before that segment of the public which has not wisely learned to stay away. *Y a des bornes, quoi! Ca exagére un peu.* Even Christian charity has its limits. Things were otherwise arranged under the old Gaelic order, before we adopted English language manners, and customs, and the usage of the 'soft word that putteth away wrath'. About fifty years after the above poem was written, a controversy arose (in verse) between one Donncha Mac Labhra, a poet, and Giollamhuire Mac Cártain, a blind harper, on the merits of music in general, and of harping in particular. Donncha threw the ball in smartly by enquiring, 'Who is this noisy corncrake?'

and Giollamhuire, wounded to the marrow of his bones, replied by stating his name, profession, and qualifications in a somewhat boastful manner (no modest violet he).

> You called me corncrake: that is wrong.
> O'Donnell and O'Neill once paid
> My music well: 'twas they who said
> 'Tis sweeter than the cuckoo's song.

After some melodious quatrains of this nature, Giollamhuire goes on to describe the importance of music in church and in Heaven; reading between the lines, it is fairly obvious that he thinks Donncha won't ever get there. He describes the efficacy of music when it comes to exorcising the devil and he ends up by saying that Donncha is an ignorant man who does not appreciate good music when he hears it. Halftime, change over, and now it's Donncha's turn to score a few points. After a short preamble in which he completely demolishes Giollamhuire, he embarks on his main argument, which is that the songs of the cuckoo and the corncrake signifying a good harvest, and the harmonious lowing of well-fed cattle, make much more pleasing music than any produced by man, and, in particular, by incompetent harpers. Herewith a few selected quatrains in rough translation:

> 'To you! To you! curds and cream!
> Sweetly sings, the cuckoo's note;
> Summer's corncrake plays by rote
> The sheaves of laden oats and wheat.'

> Finer to me lowing of cows
> At their milking twice a day,
> (Butter, cream, cheese, whey),
> Than angels' song in any house

The finest music, to my mind,
On this earth, under the sun,
Finer than silly psalmist's hum
The bull's song to his bovine brides.

Musicians are a foolish lot;
Alas for them! they must be mad,
For by their trade no luck they've had.
More profit lies in rearing stock.

Music is an empty glass
From which men drink and are destroyed:
By worthless noise are they decoyed –
Now vanished all, alas! Alas!

Thus Donncha na mBó (Donncha of the cows). Who will say that he was wrong?

8. Tuesday 1 January 1963
Young Moore's Almanac
The year 1963 is going to be one of great significance for us all. I have therefore, for the benefit of readers of this paper, compiled, from various sources, including the prophecies of Saints Malachy, Colmcille and Fachtna as well as a number of private unpublished manuscripts, a brief guide to help them through this troubled period.

January. If the wind on the first day is from the east, it bodes bad luck; if from the west, good luck. It will be cold. Avoid chapped lips and hands. Killarney, the Dingle peninsula, and the River Shannon will be bought by a Californian cartel. Heavy showers on the 27th. Berlin crisis begins.

February: St. Brigid's Day – official opening of spring. Heavy rainfall, Bord na Móna begins secret series of atomic tests in the Bog of Allen. Widespread fallout. Questions in the Dáil. Strong winds, reaching gale force, on the 16th and 17th. Repeal of the Licensing Laws on the 22nd. The railway system of C.I.E. is closed down entirely on the 24th. First spring violets appear. Entire staff of Telefís Éireann resigns. Nuclear Disarmers demonstrate outside Irish Embassies in London and Addis Ababa. Spring sowing begins. Berlin crisis continues.

March: Short heat-wave from 1st to 4th inclusive. *Ne'er cast a clout.* Due to miraculous intervention of St Patrick entire nation instanta-neously transformed into Gaelic speakers with the exception of the Government and members of the Diplomatic Corps. Heavy rainfall on the 17th. An Taoiseach resigns, March 21st. Scattery Island bought by Swiss cartel on 23rd. March 25th, President John F. Kennedy crowned king of the United Kingdom of Ireland and USA. Questions in the Dáil. Dr Noel Browne (NPD) resigns his seat. First swallows appear. Berlin crisis continues. End of financial year.

April: Showers. Censorship Board dissolved on 1st. Bord na Móna sworn enquiry begins 3rd. First primroses appear. The Independent Republic of Cork secedes formally from newly-formed United Kingdom of Ireland and USA., 5th April. Civil War begins, April 6th. Martial law in Boston, April 8th. Heavy showers on the 12th. Prime Minster Macmillan (England) resigns on the 13th, 'Sinn Féin' (100-1) wins at Fairyhouse, April 16th. Two Kerry murders are solved through the prompt and helpful co-operation of witnesses, April 19th. Blue Moon, April 20th. Russian fishing trawler arrested at Dunmore East, April 27th. Snow falls on many parts of the country, April 28th. Berlin crisis continues.

May: First day of summer. Civil war continues, with slight losses on both sides. *Queen Elizabeth* becalmed in mid-Atlantic. Bord na Móna enquiry ends, all exonerated. Springfield (Mass.) under martial law. Gales in many places. The Society for the Reformation of the GAA is formed in Magherafelt. Questions in the Dáil. Potato-sowing well under way. An Tánaiste resigns. Feis Ceoil begins. 43-pound salmon caught by nine-year-old in River Dodder. Russian space-shot fails. Strike of Department of Agriculture officials. Heavy showers on the 22nd. Berlin crisis continues. First new potatoes in the shops.

June: Bord Fáilte dissolved. Ice and snow general over the country. Civil War continues. New York under martial law. Butter subsidy removed. Resignation of the Leader of the Opposition. Strike at Fords (Dagenham) becomes general, leading to revolution in England. Fall in cattle exports. Heavy showers on the 19th. June 22nd, the Republics of England, Scotland and Wales become subdivisions of the Republic (Independent) of Cork. Dumping of eggs in Co. Monaghan. Berlin crisis continues.

***

July: Heavy rainfall. Gales in many places. Partition ends. July 12th Civil War continues. Berlin crisis continues. Light ground frost.

August: Heatwave on 2nd and 3rd followed by ice and snow. Horse Show cancelled. End of Civil War, August 5th, with capitulation of Royalist Party. Independent Cork Republic of the Western World proclaimed August 6th. Heavy rainfall on the 9th. Russia withdraws from UN on the 11th. Gaelic League branches opened Pittsburgh, Detroit, West Point and Peoria (111). Poteen still captured in Muskerry, August 23rd. Continent of South America, with Canada and Central America annexed to ICRWW on August 28th. Official opening of penal colony on the Great Blasket, August 30th. Berlin crisis continues. Mainly fair.

September. Good harvest weather. UNO dissolved. Raiders rob £16-2-11 from till of Borris-in-Ossory post office. Heavy showers on the 10th. Gaelic proclaimed official language of Cuba, Fidel Castro resigns, September 12th. Common Market countries and Scandinavia annexed by Independent Cork Republic, September 15th. Dublin Theatre Festival opens. Detectives raid Abbey Theatre, director charged with producing obscene play, cast jailed, September 20th. Dublin Theatre Festival closes. September 22nd, First Corkman landed on Mars. September 29th Berlin crisis continues. Mainly fair.

October. 'A stitch in time saves nine.' Jubilation at Farmer's Cross as Cork spaceman returns. Plumber jailed for assaulting civic guard. African continent joins Independent Cork Republic. Summit talks in Geneva, Khrushchev says: 'My grandmother was a Cork woman'. Mr Jack Lynch firm. Heavy rainfall on 15th. Oireachtas Week opens. 'Buy Cork Goods.' Plastics factory opened in Newtownmountkennedy. Berlin crisis continues. Apples should now be picked.

November. Charles de Gaulle escapes from Great Blasket, Nov. 2nd. Captured in Skibbereen, Nov. 3rd. Corkman lands on Venus, Nov. 5th. Hen lays duck egg in Co. Limerick, Nov. 9th. Heavy showers, Nov. 10th. Berlin crisis heightens, Nov. 12th. First batch of Cork colonists lands on Mars, Nov. 14th. Preparations for Cork-Venus immigration in full swing. 'Small farmer backbone of the economy,' says Minister for Agriculture. Widespread poaching in the west. Cork ultimatum to Khrushchev, Nov. 23rd. Khrushchev capitulates, Nov. 25th. Mao Tse-tung capitulates, Nov. 26th. Ice and snow in many places, giving way to rain, with occasional sunshine. 'Hasten slowly.'

December. Fate of Blasket prisoners, questions in Cork Dáil, Dec. 1st. Cork Independent World Republic declared, Dec. 2nd. Prisoners released, Dec. 4th. Gaelic proclaimed official language of World

Republic, Dec. 7th. 'Corkman's success in Venus.' Dec. 12th. Reasonable prices for turkeys. Rugby and soccer banned, Dec. 17th. Plentiful food supplies general all over the world, Dec 20th, due to intelligent planning at the Republican capital (in Cork), Dec. 25th – the snow falls gently all over the world, and everywhere on earth there is peace and contentment. Dec. 31st – we wish all our readers a bright and prosperous New Year.

9. Thursday 10 January 1963
Cambered Moujik by Jim's Jazz
[Following is the opening of a long article where Ó Riada out-Joyces Joyce!]
Coram Imperatore Eructaviti! Alas, a loon, swoony on his tod, Pavel, the Einsamkeitgeist quits the Via Reale (kumquats), and makes for the boss root (Please Do-Not Tramsferrible). Punch brother, pinch and caries, camels in extasy! Mind the steppe! Ding-ding. An sich newt as thus stood Doody with a wallow in his hind. He who laughs lost, luffs verst.

10. Saturday 26 January 1963
Everybody out of Step

> *Hispanus esuriens modo saltat, dormit Hibernus,*
> *Anglus dat lacrimas, gallus alaere canit,*

The hungry Spaniard capers in his dance.
Most sweetly sings the valiant man of France.
The Englishman does sorely cry and weep.
Whilst the Irishman doth lull his eyes to sleep.

> *I n-am na gorta nach crosta na tréithe sin,*
> *Gur damhsa is obair don pobal sin fé Philib,*
> *Ar Francach obann gur soilbh do shéideann guth,*

125

An Gall go ngoileann, 's go gcodlann a tÉireannach.

Eighteenth-century reflections on the strangeness of people who are not fortunate enough to live in Ireland, and on the very natural behaviour of the Irish themselves.

Ta rafla ag dul thart – I beg your pardon – there's a rumour going around … but before we consider the rumour, let us digress to consider its mode of conveyance. Whereas in England, according to popular legend, most rumours originate at sewing-circle meetings, in this country they generally begin in pubs. The commonest opening gambit in a conversation is 'Any news?' or 'Anything strange?' both of which questions derive from the Gaelic opening '*Aon scéal agat?*' – Have you any story? Plainly, the speaker's question is least concerned with 'hard news' – all he wants is a good story, and it is up to the other man's imagination to provide it, whether or not it tallies with the facts. Thus is art, the storyteller's art, become as necessary a part of public house life as the ubiquitously obnoxious canned music which nowadays makes the simple pint such a menace. The story usually begins *Deirtear* (it is said) or *deirtear liom* (I am told) without citing any authority to back it up. Sometimes an irate seeker after truth, boorishly maddened by this reluctance to render the facts their due, will say, '*Ni raibh sa scéal ach dubhairt-bean-liom-go-ndubhairt-bean-leí.*' (All that was in the story was 'a woman told me that a woman told her'). But to get back to my rumour.

***

I am told that we may not, after all, be going into the Common Market, and that as a result there is weeping, wailing and gnashing of teeth in high places. This is surely a very childish reaction. If we examine the matter, we will see that we are far better off out of it. Other commentators have discussed the advisability, or otherwise, of entering the Common Market, using old-fashioned arguments based on politics or economics. These are without significance in this present era; the only valid argument is based on the axiom, 'Nations, like men, may be judged by what they eat.'

During the last three months of 1962, hordes of hungry foreigners swooped down on this country, ostensibly just tourists on shooting holidays. Their behaviour, however, was at variance with their disguise. Of the 400-odd foreign shooters who invaded County Wicklow alone (most of them Frenchmen with a few Germans thrown in), I have to report that, as well as shooting those birds commonly regarded as game, they also shot vast numbers of thrushes, blackbirds, sparrows, wrens, even crows. Some of these they devoured on the spot, but by far the greater number they sent back to their needy relations on the Continent, hygienically wrapped in polythene bags. It was when I heard about this that I formulated what modesty forbids me to hope will be referred to as 'Ó Riada's Axiom' – that nations, like men, may be judged by what they eat.

The French, to all outward appearances a reasonably civilised and intelligent nation, betray themselves by eating, as well as small birds, frogs, snails and other abominations. This is merely the outward symptom of a deep-seated racial trauma – they are obviously not to be trusted. The Germans, for centuries, have had an obsession with sausages. This obsession dominates every aspect of their lives and thought, even to the extent of governing their choice of pets – that curious looking Dachshund, for example. The Belgians are addicted to eating horseflesh, preferably of Irish provenance. (It is interesting to note that in this country horseflesh is fed mainly to beagles, a possible corruption, by metathesis, of the word Belgae?) The Italians as string-eaters – the literal meaning of 'spaghetti' is 'little strings'. I would suggest, as a possible subject for research by future scholars, that Dante's vision of Hell can, to a large extent, be attributed to over-indulgence in string-eating.

These, then, are the Common Market countries, with all the

horror of their diet. But, if we wish we can apply the axiom to other nations just as easily. The Russians, for instance, must be very short of food if they have to come to Ireland to steal their fish.

Any nation that could even contemplate the very idea of 'borscht' – cabbage soup (!), is automatically suspect. The Americans will eat no meat that has not been frozen for at least six months, whereupon it is simultaneously flavourised, deodorised, tenderised, and finally gobbled up too quickly. The English deliberately cultivate stomach disorders and bad tempers by eating greasy mutton and hard buns, as anyone who has passed through Euston station can testify. And the Chinese, of course, have passed the borderline with their thousand-year old egg and all the rest of it. Are we the only sane nation left on earth? I'm afraid we are Ichabod.

The world's peace, at the moment, depends on a very precarious balance which could be upset very easily. Our government is dismayed at the thought that if we do not enter the Common Market, we will not have anybody to whom to export our prime Irish beef. This fact in itself is an example of how far the present insanity has spread. They should be glad! If these foreigners sank their teeth into a nice juicy sirloin or fillet steak cut from prime Irish beef, the shock of good food would prove too much for their already unbalanced menu and they would immediately go berserk and start to eat each other (a most unwholesome diet.) War would break out in all directions and we would be invaded by innumerable kinds of undesirables. Let reason prevail! Should we enter the Common Market and allow ourselves to take the above course, the name of Ireland will be forever black. Should we, on the other hand, decide to take the harder road posterity will bless our name as the saviours of the human race. Let us look before we leap. Not everybody is ready for tripe and drisheen.

11. Monday 11 February 1963

Your Humble and Obedient

In common with the vast majority of Irishmen, I find myself utterly incapable of writing letters. It is odd that a nation whose main recreation is talking should find the epistolary form of communication so repugnant. I envy those friends of mine who are able to answer letters on the day they arrive, but suspect them, secretly, of being foreigners. I always begin the day with the best of intentions; having scrutinised the letters, I resolve to answer them – immediately, but something (the *deus ex machina*, I suppose) always intervenes. When I look at the pile of unanswered letters, some of them more than three months old, I often comfort myself with the thought that unanswered letters, if left long enough, usually answer themselves. (Sometimes this has a rather hollow sound, like the saying 'Too much money makes unhappiness').

This letter-writing inability of Irishmen must be of fairly recent origin. Our parents, or at least our grandparents, needed no encouragement to harass their friends and relations with long, involved messages written in flowing copperplate. A great-aunt of mine, famous in her own parish for her sharp-tongued aphorisms (two of them were: of children – ''Tis bad with them, but worse without them', and 'Visitors and fish smell after the third day') used to spend a minimum of two hours a day writing letters to all and sundry – making life hell for her correspondents who had to answer them. It is probably just as well that she has gone to her reward.

In those days letter-writing was the act of the common man, practised by everybody. Each word was considered and weighed in its relation to the context, and the whole letter was carefully composed with regard to the prevailing literary standards. Nowadays the common man picks up the telephone, and the most celebrated letters of our day are those exchanged between the politicians who like to regard themselves as statesmen: Macmillan, Kruschev, Kennedy, de Gaulle, Adenaur and the rest. Such letters are invariably badly-composed, lacking in style,

threatening in tone, and in general prolix, inelegant, bombastic, churl-
ish – obviously the work of semi-literates who would be all the better
for a good clouting in the fifth class of any Irish national school. Faugh!
Or to be more precise, fie!

One of the most charming (and moving) letters I have ever seen
was written by the Gaelic poet, Piaras Mac Gearailt in 1769. Piaras
came from near Knockadoon in east Cork, and at the time this letter
was written, was about sixty years of age. The letter was to accompany
a gift of a book in manuscript form which he had copied himself, and
was sent to the young wife of a friend of his, one Creagh Butler. My
rough translation cannot adequately convey the elegance of the original
Gaelic prose, but the sentiments expressed are human, and universal.

A.D. 1769. Herewith, my dear, gentle, sweet, graceful, clever,
mannerly, womanly friend, this mean, humble little present,
which I promised you for the use and pastime of that noble, splen-
did, fresh-hearted man, that is, Creagh Butler, and you would have
had this little collection long before now but for my being sick and
rheumy, keeping to my bed and my room for a whole season, since
I had the honour of last seeing you at Ahnakishy near by Mallow,
in the house of my old and cherished friend, gentle Piaras de
Nogla. I trust that the affable Butler will not hold in contempt this
poor gathering or collection of mine, since it was with good intentions and in all honour towards you and to your generous, fortunate, courtly companion that I now took it in hands, in my sixti-
eth year, to write so much in one week, and as well as that I am
not yet free from the pangs of illness – rheumatism, and several
other ailments which have been chipping at me for some time;
these are responsible for making this little bit of writing so botchy
and full of mistakes. Indeed, it is my sick depression, my grief, my
heartscald, that I am not again at the age of ten and twenty years,
with a regular secure estate of ten thousand guineas a year, that I

130

might hope for the merit, the honour, the good fortune, the life's pleasure and the heart's ease of your accepting as a gift that part which you stole from me long since, namely, my heart, for I am overflowing with an abundant affection, lively, burning, everlasting, for your person, your dear face, your look, your many virtues and your gentle behaviour: and in any case, it won't be long until I will have the pleasure of seeing you again, since I am, with much respect, sincerity, humility, continuing sympathy, and lifelong love, dear gracious lady –

Your prisoner and your servant, continually miserable, mournful and grieving until I see again your bright shining face. Piaras Mac Gearailt, High-Sheriff (of the Court of Poetry) of Munster.'

As if such a letter in itself were not enough, Piaras subjoined to it a poem in her praise. This is a very far cry from the kind of letter with which we are all familiar – I mean the Civil Service type of letter:

A Chara,
Thank you for your letter of January 32, the contents of which have been noted and will receive our consideration,
Is mise, le meas,
Signature (illegible).

It is one of the disasters of our time that official letter-writing is practically the only branch of the art that survives, apart from the note to the milkman. However, even these, in time, will die out, and only a few eccentrics will continue to write to each other, thereby saving us all a great deal of trouble. Three cheers for progress.

12. TUESDAY 19 FEBRUARY 1963

LHUDE SING CUCU!

One last despairing plea, in the hope of bringing the weather to its senses: never mind about the snows of yesteryear, just tell us, where is the spring? Has it disappeared forever from the world, will it be only a memory from now on, like that faint, almost-forgotten whiff of youth, or the sweet apple-smell in the drawer of an old empty cupboard? I'm afraid so. A new ice age is upon us, and any day now we will hear the rumbling of glaciers in the north. But what about the future?

The year is 1970. The time is what used to be described humorously as the spring. Amidst a tinkling of little bells, the Taoiseach (Mr C. Haughey, F.G.) draws up in a reindeer-drawn sleigh outside Leinster House. He is wearing a heavy, green-dyed mink coat, a black fur hat, and a pair of the new Italian snowshoes, trimmed in ermine. As he hurries through the great doors, a worried-looking official from Bord na Móna comes up to him and whispers briefly in his ear. (Something about a plague of polar bears on Boora Bog). The Taoiseach dismisses him with a nod and a gracious wave of his hand, hurrying onwards. The warm air of the Dáil restaurant strikes him like a blow in the face. Inside, all is cheerfulness and good company. The huge samovar, a recent import from the east, huffs and bubbles merrily. Around it, a group of deputies from the south and west are discussing in lively tones the All-Ireland Indoor Croquet Final between Belmullet and Magherafelt. The Tánaiste, clad in a maroon quilted dressing-gown (lined with sable), sips a glass of scented lemon tea, and chats to a few cronies about the possibility of forming an All-Girl Army Band. In a far corner of the room, the Ceann Comhairle is reciting melodious quatrains in praise of skating. A lovely scene indeed. But where is the leader of the Opposition? If the Taoiseach but knew. He is sitting on a camp stool on the frozen surface of the pond in St Stephen's Green, watching officials from the Fisheries Department fishing through holes in the ice, while his Party Whip beside him strums a melancholy tune on his balalaika. The news is not too good – there is a strike threatened by the CIE droshky-drivers. Last night the new Director-General of Telifís Éireann was eaten by wolves on his way home from a press conference. This will mean more trouble – how unpleasant to have to be eternally asking questions in the Dáil!

***

An old story tells of a dispute between a fox and a hawk as to which of them had experienced the coldest night. The fox described a very bad night indeed when the milk was frozen in the farmers' churns, and so on. 'Ah,' said the hawk, 'that wasn't a patch on the cold night when I picked the eye out of a salmon's head. It was a night in May which froze very suddenly. The salmon jumped up in the water to catch a fly, and while he was rising, the water froze, so that I was able to pick his eye out while he was stuck there in the ice.' It seems to me that that could have happened almost any night recently.

But maybe the spring will come in the end. As a quatrain has it:

Ní i n-aon áird fhanas an ghaoth, cé go mbíonn fraoch ar an sín:
ní mhaireann anfadh do ghnáth, is bídh an mhuir tráth go min.

The wind must change from time to time.
Even though it's wild and harsh:
Storms blow themselves out at last –
The sea, sometimes, in peace must lie.

'With the coming of Spring, the day will be stretching,' sang
        Raftery,
'And Saint Brigid's Day over, I soon will set sail:
For since I first thought it, my feet will be stepping
Till they stand in the middle of Mayo's green fields.'

133

The spring will surely come, with the young buds on the trees and the small flowers smiling at the sun; the birds singing and making their nests; trout leaping in the rivers, lambs frisking on the meadows; and it won't be long until we hear the cuckoo's call, a minor third ringing through the waking woods. Poets have always sung the spring, from the English Chaucer to Tennyson and Bridges. Remember Thomas Nash – 'Spring, the sweet spring, the year's pleasant King ...' Or the German poet Hölderlin who used spring as a synonym for youth:

> *Das Angenehme dieser Welt hab'ich genossen,*
> *Die Jugendfreuden sind wie lang, wie lang verflossen:*
> *April, und Mai, und Junius sind ferne.*
> *Ich bin nicht mehr, ich lebe nicht meh gerne.*

> The pleasures of this world were once my knowing,
> But joyful youth was swiftly, swiftly going:
> April, and May, and June were once my treasure –
> I am no more pent by Time's fleeting measure.

Or, by contrast, the medieval Irish monk who wrote in Gaelic on the margin of his manuscript:

> A leafy ledge above me hangs,
> A blackbird's song comes pouring out –
> My lined book and myself beneath
> His metred singing, elegant.
> Here, too, the sweet-voiced cuckoo sings
> His jovial song in the green-cloaked bush;
> I thank the Lord who cherishes
> Me here, within this pleasant wood.

This is not too far from the old English *Sumer is icumen in, lhude sing cucu.* But during this past winter I have been tempted more than once to recall Ezra Pound's parody of the same lines:

Winter is icummen in
Lhude sing Goddamn,
Raineth drop and staineth slop
And how the wind doth ramm!
Sing Goddamm.
Chorus, me boys!

13. 18 MARCH 1963
PATTER OF TINY HOOVES

It is true that children are a blessing. It is equally true that there are no unmixed blessings. Hence we can by synthesis infer that children (especially the neighbours' children; often, alas, our own), may sometimes be classed with the minor demons. It is finally true that Irish children are surpassed for devilishness only by the children of foreigners, mainly American and English. Everybody knows that the coming generation is not a patch on the preceding one (our own generation). Why is this thus? It is extremely difficult to understand how people of our generation, who as children themselves were well-mannered, obedient and considerate, could produce a generation of delinquents whose conduct frequently verges on the bestial. (In parenthesis I might mention that a friend of mine, who subsequently obtained a high position as an educationalist, when he was once approached by an elderly lady soliciting funds for the Society for the Prevention of Cruelty to Children, snarled in reply, 'Madam, I always make it a point of being cruel to children!' Stout fellow, that was the spirit!)

About a thousand years ago, before this civilised country was thrust into barbarism by woad-painted barbarians from across the Irish Sea, we had solved this problem of children ourselves in a very elegant way. The solution was, quite simply, the fosterage system. This meant that Parent A sent his children to Parent B for rearing and education, while Parent B countered by sending his children to Parent A. This meant that Parent A could chastise (or beat the lard out of) the children of the house, without being emotionally upset at seeing his own childish tear-streaked image staring reproachfully back at him. Secondly, it meant that Parent A had to return the children in good condition, fat and rosy, and bulging with education, otherwise Parent 'B' would, at the very least, hold a sworn enquiry. Thirdly, and very importantly, it meant that Parent B's children were hostages for the good behaviour of Parent A's children, and vice versa. A wonderful system, full of a beauty and simplicity expressed otherwise only in such things as Pythagoras' Theorem or the Third Law of Thermodynamics. And with what did our overlords, having destroyed it, replace it? With chaos, insubordination, and back answers. No wonder the Common Market wouldn't have us.

It is useless now, however, to complain that our system was destroyed by naked savages from England. We must, instead, strive to find a solution for the problem as it exists among us today. Most experts agree that some form of counter-irritant will help towards this solution. Some have suggested using the back of a round, flat hairbrush. Others are more in favour of the wooden spoon, accompanying each blow with a short rotary motion of the upper arm. *The Irish Parent* (quarterly) of February 29th. 1903, advocates the use of a tennis racket. This, to my mind, is surely for the few, and perhaps a bit too fanciful for the common man. Other suggestions include hurleys, small ornamental brass coal-shovels, ping-pong bats (these produce quite a musical sound), fish-slices, and, in extreme cases, banjos with strings removed. On no account should objects with sharp or jagged edges be used – the aim is to counter-irritate, not to wound. It should also be borne in mind that punishment needs always to be accompanied by precept. I therefore append a short list of useful sentences, any of which may be used, according to circumstances; the chosen sentences should be repeated with each counter-irritatory stroke.

1. 'If you do that again, I'll murder you!' (The stroke should accompany the syllable 'mur', which is heavily accented.
2. 'You will not refer to your father again as a superannuated old buffer!' (Here the stroke falls on 'buff'.)
3. 'False teeth do not float!'
4. 'For the forty-third time, I repeat, let this be a warning to you!'
5. 'This hurts me more than it hurts you!' (Stroke to coincide with 'you', heavily accented.)
6. 'Manners maketh the man!'
7. 'How dare you speak to your mother in that tone of voice! I will not tolerate that kind of strong language from impudent puppies who have been taught better. Remember that in future, sir!' (Stroke to fall on 'fu'.)

These sentences, as you can see, may be readily memorised, and I trust that the foregoing may be of some help and guidance in the matter of corrective treatment for this greatest disease of our time.

Finally, should all else fail, I can only recommend the recitation, in calm, equable tones, of that admirable set of verses devised by Cormac Mac Airt, High King of Ireland, for the edification of his son. These have come down to us via oral transmission, and were known in the eighteenth century as *Comhairle na Barrscolóige dá mhac*. Here are some selected quatrains, in my own rough translation:

My son, here's my advice,
My lion of Art's breeding,
Complaints must be heard twice,
First one, then t'other heeding.

Be neither hard nor soft
Though friends never forsaking;

Fight not unless you must,
But then be first in striking.

When in the market place,
Do not condemn the pauper;
Nor idiot hold in scorn –
No wise man yet was faultless

At drinking be not first,
Nor at your elders jeering;
Respect a poor man's thirst –
No good is got from sneering.

Beware the sleeky smart
The playboy, cheaply witty;
Prefer the noble heart
That knows both love and pity.

Should this final parental remedy, the musical recitation of these melodious verses, fail, there is only one course of action left. Send for the Gardai, and a happy bow-wow to one and all.

14. 31 JULY 1963
PLAIN WORDS

At this stage, I suppose there is no use in complaining to Mr Dillon about compulsory English in schools. He has the bit too firmly between his teeth. I wish to register my objection to compulsory English, just the same. English is, in fact, a highly deficient language, and if it were not for the work of various dedicated scholars like myself, who are constantly revising and refining it, it would long ago have become obsolete as a vehicle of communication.

Herewith, then, the latest list of revisions suggested by the Friends of the English Language, Great Blasket Branch (of which I have the honour to be chairman).

1. National Collective Nouns:
A gargle of Frenchmen,
A pot of Chinamen,
A muddle of Englishmen.
A peal of Italians,
A pudding of Germans,
A turn-up of Swedes.
A thump of Russians,
A stand of Poles,
A clutch of Czechs.
A welt of Spaniards,
A hoist of Yanks,
A gobble of Turks.

What about ourselves? Obvious. A totter of Irishmen.

Further additions to this list will appear from time to time in the Society's Monthly Bulletin (Five Guineas per annum, post free).

***

2. Demotic English or Spoken English v. Written English
This controversy continues to arouse enthusiasm and interest. At the last meeting on the island, a Dublin member proposed that in the Dublin Metropolitan Area, written Sa'da' be substituted for written Saturday, and he made the point that in the D.M.A. spoken Sa'da' receives majority usage. (The first apostrophe in Sa'da' represents a glottal stop or click..) The suggestion was referred to our Committee For Spoken Usage, due to meet in September, 1964.

3. Additions to the Supplement of the Society's Dictionary of Contemporary Usage:

[I have ommitted this list, which was considered libellous. T. Ó C]

4. Members' Correspondence and Editorial comment.

One of our student members, a certain Mr Haughey (student members are admitted to the Society on payment of half of the subscription paid by fully-fledged members), writes:

'A Chara, I have made up my mind to withdraw from the Society (sic!) as I feel I am wasting my time in it, been now fully in command of the English language. What's more, I was very desattsfied with your decision on whether to pronounce Parnell Parnell or Parnell. Please refund my subscription in full, as I have now desided to take up the Irish language. Is mise le mass', etc.

(The best of luck to ex-member Haughey in his new venture. We trust his struggles with Irish are better-rewarded than his former struggles with English. Once again, beast wishes!

***

5. A message From the President of the Great Blasket Friends Of The English Language:

'Fellow members and fellow English-speakers – by the time some of you read this, in what far-distant lands, it will once more be spring. Spring, a time of hope for us all, a time for all young things, a time of hope for all those, no longer young, who have survived the cruel winter. And surely it will be once more a time of hope for our glorious heritage, our silver tongue, our long-neglected English language! The bitter and savage onslaught made by our former colonial and subject peoples on our language has been a blow from which it is difficult to recover. Jealousy and resentment have tried to corrupt our language. No longer do we hear 'nought' (or 'naught'); the abomination of 'zero' is on everyone's lips. Nowadays, men of affairs are 'businessmen' who 'do deals'; people spend their time 'ringing up' other people. The language, it would seem, is in a parlous state. But courage! There is still hope! Hope, a light shining through the darkness, a gleam of silver, lining this cloud of despair. Let us put our shoulders to the wheel and our noses to the grindstone. Let us take courage from those whom we presume to lead, namely, the lower classes. Let them be an example to each and every one of us, for they have kept faith. They alone have been true to the real glory of our language, those beautiful, short, monosyllabic, ancient Anglo-Saxon words, the truest English, so wonderfully expressive of our great cause and ourselves I could say more but – words fail me.'

CHAPTER 12

CÚIL AODHA

Ó Riada's Dublin friends felt his life as a composer was finished
when he left the city to live in Cúil Aodha in autumn 1963, to
take up his new post as a lecturer in the music department in
University College Cork. They thought it bad enough that he should
leave the capital city but to go to a small townland where he would
have no intellectual stimulation such as he had enjoyed in Dublin
appalled them. Where would he get the inspiration a composer needs?
What was in store for him? Worse still, he had no telephone to link
him with life in the big city and he didn't reply to letters!

Ó Riada was simply acting as he always had done – changing to
something new and turning his back on the past, however pleasant it
had been. This tendency towards change was evident in every aspect of
his life, even in hunting, fishing, boating, or in making model airplanes
that he could fly, as a pastime. Everything for Seán had its allotted span
and when that was over, it did not exist for him any more. Peadar, his
son, had often noticed this characteristic. He saw it as something Seán
had inherited from his mother, Julia: it implied that you should do your
utmost to reach the top in whatever project you might be involved.
When you had done your very best and completed the task, you should

face the next challenge. That was how Julia reared her family.

Local priest Father Donncha Ó Conchúir told how the Ó Riada's came to live in Cúil Aodha: he remembered meeting Seán one day in summer 1963 in Ballyferriter, when the family were living in Seán de h-Óra's house. Ó Riada was returning from the butcher's with a parcel of meat under his arm. They had a short chat and went their separate ways but soon afterwards Seán contacted the priest to tell him that he had just obtained a teaching post in University College Cork but did not wish to live in the city. His first preference, he said, would be to stay where they were in Kerry, but that was too far away from Cork to allow him to travel up and down for lectures. He asked Father Donncha Ó Conchúir if there was any hope of buying or renting a house in Cúil Aodha.

The priest knew that Máire Ní Cheocháin was selling her house there, so Ó Riada, accompanied by Seán de h-Óra and Séamus Ó Cíomháin, went to see her in Cork. By the time they returned that evening the deal was settled: Ó Riada was the new owner. Some time later he went to Cúil Aodha with a few of his Kerry friends to clear fences and his father came out from Cork to help with the painting and general decoration of the house.

When the Ó Riada family were moving house, they stopped to ask directions from a man working at the roadside. He was Seán Mac Suibhne, a former Republican and noted Irish speaker. Ó Riada asked the way in Irish and was pointed in the right direction for his new house, but years later, when Mac Suibhne had become a very good friend of the family, he told them the full story behind their first meeting. It seems that Mac Suibhne had a high regard for an earlier owner of the house, Dónal Ó Ceocháin, who was credited with being responsible for keeping the Irish language alive in Cúil Aodha in past times. When Mac Suibhne heard that the house had been sold to strangers who, he thought, would have no respect for Cúil Aodha traditions nor be able to speak Irish, he decided that they would not remain more than a single night in the house: he had a plan to banish them. However, when he realised who the strangers were and especially when he heard Ó Riada's polished Irish, he changed his mind completely. Of course, the newcomers were not really strangers, for Julia Creedon, Seán's mother and her family, hailed from west Cork.

Ruth was the first to get to know the people of the district, since the five children attended the local school and she would meet people on her shopping expeditions and through her friends Bean Uí Mhuineacháin and Máire John Ní Shúilleabháin, who helped her with household chores. Some of the locals were surprised to hear the Ó Riada children speaking Irish as, even though Cúil Aodha was officially in the Gaeltacht, many families did not value their Irish sufficiently to pass it on to their children. This changed later and some people give credit to Ó Riada for that.

Seán had a habit of going in to Williams' pub every morning and would meet people there but he never went at night when the locals were there. So it took him a while to get to know them, though he was already acquainted with those who attended annual Oireachtas competitions in Dublin, including an older singer, Mícheál Ó Súilleabháin (Mikey), to whom he was related.

Tadhg Ó Mulláin, a widower who lived alone, became very friendly with the family and visited them nearly every day. He was a fund of knowledge on folklore and local traditions and Seán learned a lot from him about such things. Tadhg's expertise covered many areas, including farming and he became the family's official adviser on matters of gardening and even of house repairs. He would later become the chairman of their musical evenings in the house, before the choir, Cór Cúil Aodha, came into being. Seán used to tell the story of Tadhg and an Englishman who was questioning him about Ireland's fight for freedom. The Englishman doubted that a poor downtrodden group of country people could chase out the English who, at the time, had a large Empire. 'I'll tell you,' said Tadhg, jokingly, 'it was with big sticks and stockings full of shit that we got rid of them – believe you me!'

It was Ó Riada who recommended to the priest, Father Donncha Ó Conchúir, that he should bring a few local lads together to sing in the church. They began about a year after Seán's arrival, one Thursday night towards the end of 1964. Only then did the majority of them get to know Seán well. Father Donncha Ó Conchúir told me that it was curiosity about this strange newcomer in their midst that brought some of them to the first practice. They remained to learn music from him and, even though they did not appreciate it at the time, they were to have a major influence on Seán.

Seán was moving closer and closer to native traditions during this period in Cúil Aodha. He felt that local ways were very important and was always open to what Tadhg Ó Mulláin taught him about local customs and culture. He delved deeper into the work of the Munster poets. It was no surprise to the family that much of this work was done in the toilet, where he could spend hours reading and singing.

It was felt at first that Cór Cúil Aodha should sing a few hymns at evening benediction, once a month. Towards this end they learned *O Salutaris, Tantum Ergo* and *Caoineadh na dTrí Muire*. Seán insisted they should understand every word of the Latin and they spent a long time finding a good translation, in their best Irish, for the Latin text. *Mo Ghrá-sa mo Dhia* was the next piece to be added to their repertoire and then Tadhg recommended an old verse that would be suitable as a recessional hymn after mass. They soon had a hymn for the beginning of mass as well as *Ár n-Athair* (Our Father), another of Seán's compositions. When they added his communion hymn, they were close to what we now know as the Ó Riada mass. Seán was always very careful about ensuring that everyone was at ease in the hymns before introducing new material.

This first mass was firmly grounded in the Irish singing tradition. It was influenced by traditional singers such as Seán de h-Óra' and Mort Ó Sé, particularly in *A Rí an Domhnaigh* and *Gile Mo Chroí*.

While Seán's mass, as sung by Cór Cúil Aodha every week in the local church, was widely welcomed, some of the congregation were not happy about any kind of singing at mass, as it interfered with their prayers and was distracting them from their rosary!

Ó Riada was undoubtedly spiritual, in the broadest sense of the term, at this time. His notion of *An Naisiún Gaelach* (the Irish nation) seemed founded on a mixture of spiritual beliefs and native traditions. It was something he often brought up in conversation and he was turning against the kind of life he had been involved with in Dublin. He used to invite his city friends to forget European art and music and come to Cúil Aodha to experience *An Naisiún Gaelach*, to which he was so committed. Seán said that he was finished with European music and in future would only be concerned with Irish music in 1968 or, at the latest, 1969. He always maintained, in any discussion on the future of Ireland, that the Irish language was central to everything, both in the general cultural sphere and in the ordinary life of the people. For Seán this was more than a talking point in academic circles: it had become a reality that affected every phase of his own life.

Seán had strong opinions on the North and what should be done to solve its problems. His solution was generally one of force. His opinions were not only simplistic, but dangerous and reckless – those of a person who had never lived in the North and who had not experienced its problems at first hand. Ruth had difficulty restraining him in 1969 when the Northern troubles broke out in earnest, as he very much wanted to take his gun and fight for his own Gaelic nation on the barricades of Belfast.

Looking at another aspect of Seán's character, one might say that in ways he was a lazy person who needed either to be pushed or inspired to complete a task. There had always been professional colleagues to do that in Dublin - but not in Cúil Aodha. He was glad to take life easy there and enjoy it. He had his gun and his fishing rod for sport, a fine house on the bank of the Sullane River, a permanent and not too demanding post in the University – and a pile of unanswered letters!

However, his letters give another picture of Seán, as someone who was involved in many projects during the Cúil Aodha years, from 1963 to 1971. Many were from the Donald Langdon Agency in London, concerning films for which Ó Riada was being asked to provide music. The first, in 1964, concerns the film *Young Cassidy*, mentioning a fee of £300 on signature of preliminary agreement. Correspondence dated November 1964 mentions two enclosed fees – one of £300 for delivery of the copied musical parts and one of a further £300 for completion of the recording. Subsequently, in March 1965, a further letter to the effect that Robbins Music Corporation Ltd., 'to whom the music rights in Mr O'Riada's music were assigned, wished to engage a lyric writer in USA to write a lyric for the main theme tune, for exploitation in connection with the film ... 50% of these royalties to Mr O'Riada.'

Seán's lack of a telephone was a source of considerable frustration to many who were looking for immediate replies. One telegram from the BBC read: 'Please telephone Langham 4468, extension 3810. Thursday, March 7 at 3.30. Reverse charge. Cleverdon.' It was not uncommon for appointments to be made for Seán to be at the local post office at a particular time to await calls from abroad.

It was not all serious music that was being produced in Cúil Aodha at that time. The Molly Neville Agency, on behalf of Arks Ltd., sent a cheque for £350 for a 'Players Navy Cut jingle'. It is surprising that Seán was writing an advertising jingle for cigarettes.

In March and April 1965 there were letters from Charlie Davis, Encino, California and Dublin Productions Ltd., about Seán's music for the Kennedy film. Evidently Seán had recommended the song *Carrigdhoun* for shots of Kennedy leaving Shannon, but Davis suggested it was a bit sad and they should move quickly to a rousing number like *Kelly the boy from Killane*, so that the scene would finish on an up-beat. Davis added what he called a personal note: 'Let me know within the next week or so how you want your credit lines on screen – Musical Director ... or Score by ... or Music composed and arranged by ...' Just a week later he wrote: 'Your phone call took me by surprise: thought it was Peter Owens: my shock at May 15th. recording date ...' Obviously, Seán in this case was, unusually for him, way ahead of schedule.

A letter dated 14 October 1965 from Gerard Victory, who was then Deputy Director of Music, sought a new arrangement of the National Anthem for full symphony orchestra for television in Easter week 1966, offering a fee of £60, which Seán accepted in a subsequent letter, dated October 22: 'commencing work on the arrangement immediately and should be able to let you have completed score before November 15. The fee, while it is not staggeringly magnificent, is acceptable to me.' Victory had also asked him on another occasion about *Nomos No. 2* as an 'Italia Prize' entry and wanted to know the copyright situation concerning the text translation Seán had used.

Seán's television series, *Music and Man*, was transmitted early in 1967 and there was a contract among his papers for four programmes, with a fee of £60 per programme and expenses of £8-11-0. A programme report gave listeners' reaction to the sixth in the series, *Lays and Love Songs*, directed by Seán Ó Mórdha and transmitted on 27 February.

'Summary: This programme, which received the slightly above average Reaction Index of 66, was well – if not enthusiastically, received by viewers. Seán Ó Riada was highly praised for his comprehensive knowledge and the excellent presentation of his material, and the selection of music was also considered very appropriate as an illustration of the points he was making, as well as being quite enjoyable in itself. As a series, *Music and Man* was described as interesting, educational and enjoyable.'

Among Seán's papers there was a long official letter from Gerard Victory (by now Director of Music) in 1968, commissioning the three de Valera works. The RTE specification for the commission was:

a) Elegy for speakers, soloists, choir and symphony orchestra of not less than 30 or more than 40 minutes. £500 for score, not later than March 15 1969. Elegy would be appropriate in text and musical content for use as a tribute to a deceased Irish patriot and statesman.

b) A Requiem Mass suitable for performance at the obsequies of a deceased statesman: a capella choir: linking passages for tradition- al instruments. Fee £300. Score not later than April 1, 1969. (At least 20 minutes of music.)

c) Requiem (Military Band) March and Pipe Lament. £200 offered. It is understood that this work has been substantially com- pleted.

There were various letters from the BBC concerning music from Seán and fees. Peter Luke was in contact many times about the film about Seán that he was making. It was transmitted on 29 December 1966 on BBC2.

Michael Emerson, director of the Belfast Festival, was in frequent contact with Seán in summer 1967 about Seán's forthcoming appear- ance at the Belfast Festival, where he was to conduct the premiere of his *Nomos No. 6*. Emerson promised £300 if Seán remained at the Festival for three days. Emerson was getting nervous in July when he sent an urgent telegram asking for a photo and biography.

There was a handwritten letter in Irish from Fionán Mac Coluim about his magazine, *An Saol Gaelach*, saying that Dónal Ó Móráin had told him that Seán would co-operate with Gael Linn in helping to publish the magazine. In a list of his publications for 1965, Ó Riada claimed both the editing and publishing of *An Saol Gaelach*. On the same document he claimed, in respect of his *Ailliliú* programmes: music arranged, programmes scripted, filmed and edited by Seán Ó

1965?

Riada. That seems to have been a busy year for Seán, with radio and TV programmes almost every month, involving *Fleadh Ceoil an Radio, Reacaireacht an Riadaigh* and *Ailliliú*. His *Young Cassidy* music was recorded in that year by Sinfonia of London and *Nomos No. 2* was premiered by the RESO, conducted by Tibor Paul, with Robert Moulton, baritone. The Radio Éireann Symphony Orchestra were playing Ó Riada music again, later in the year, when Seán conducted his own *Rhapsody of a River*.

Various letters were sent from Desmond Moran of Moran and Ryan concerning two companies Seán was proposing to set up in August 1965. These were named in a letter from Seán to Moran & Ryan in November of that year as 1.) *Seán Ó Riada Teoranta* and 2.) *Draíon-Scannáin Teoranta*. Many years later, soon after Seán's death, there was a letter from the Inspector of Taxes concerning Dracon *(sic)* Films.

A letter from the Union of Composers of the USSR, dated 30 March 1965, contained an invitation for Seán Ó Riada and his wife to visit Russia. It was forwarded to him with a covering note (dated 7 April) from Frank Edwards, secretary of the Irish-Soviet Friendship Society. Another letter, dated 25 March, from Frank Coffey of External Affairs, mentioned possible political objections to acceptance, but seemed to think there should not be any. He did not seem sure about the possible effect of the visit on the granting of a USA visa to Ó Riada in the future. Seán accepted the invitation on 26 April, mentioning the possibility of a date in August of that year.

In this period in Cúil Aodha Ó Riada was drinking quite a lot, though he rarely seemed to be drunk. Ronnie McShane reckons he and Ruth were the only two who could tell from his eyes whether he was drunk or not and they claimed to know from his skin-tone whether or not he was angry! His son Peadar saw him drunk on only two occasions – once when he fell, on his way into the house and the children heard him swearing, and on another occasion when he was driving back with the family from Kenmare, where he kept his boat. Whatever happened, he drove into the ditch at the side of the road. Peadar was shocked and said to Ruth, in a loud voice: 'Seán is drunk.' Ruth was angry with the poor lad, who burst out crying and, as he still remembers, continued crying for two days.

Peadar said that Ruth and Seán were very much in love and would often kiss at home, much to the embarrassment of their children. At other times, they could be seen kissing on the street in Cork, something their children considered out of place.

He remembers the various crazes that struck Seán in those days and the urgency with which he followed each new fad – at least until the newness had gone from it. Boating was what he spent most time and effort on. He would buy every boating magazine he could find. On one occasion he bought a book about boats for Peadar's birthday but, even though Peadar was interested in boats, he had no doubt that Seán had really bought it for himself. It was the same with model airplanes: the Ó Riada children would all get model airplanes as birthday presents, whilst their father still suffered from plane-fever. They used to have regular boat trips from Kenmare, before he purchased an old hooker in Galway, in which he intended they would go right around Ireland. But, like all Seán's pastimes, that did not last very long either. It was the same with the dogs: Seán was happy they had a real Irish wolfhound, but it was left to Peadar to clear up after it.

His daughter Rachel remembers many things about her father: his kindness and pleasure in playing with children; his inconsistency in making strict rules of behaviour for them, which he promptly forgot next day; the games he used to play with them at table – when he would announce that anyone who would speak, show their teeth or laugh was the *amadán* (fool). They would have to continue eating, quietly and seriously until someone would break the silence with an unrestrained laugh. At other times, they would not be allowed to say a 'yes' or 'no' in conversation, while Seán would be doing his best to coax the forbidden words from them.

Rachel remembers the fear she had that her father would die young. She was religious and would often pray it would not happen. Once, she brought her brother Eoin upstairs to say the rosary for that intention. Seán did not receive in their local church, which was a cause of great concern to Rachel, as she was taught at school it was a sin not to receive communion at least once a year. She used to pray he would go, but she stopped that when she realised that if he did, God might call him up to heaven because he was such a good person – and then she would be left without a father. She continued to pray, however, that he would be left on earth until he was 100 years old, though she could not imagine her father as an old man.

When a small dog Seán had brought home to her from Cork was killed, he promised to get her a horse for Christmas that year, which he did, along with a saddle, a hat, jodhpurs and all she needed. She remembers too that she knew, even before he mentioned the horse, what he was going to get her. She took riding lessons and her father promised to buy her a hunting horse when she was sixteen, but poor Seán was dead by then. She remembers the many Christmas presents they received each year.

Rachel was sent to school to Coláiste Íde in Dingle. She felt there was a bit of snobbery in both that and the horse riding - at least in her father's eyes – and she knew he liked that. He wanted her to look well at all times and she remembers him, one evening, combing her hair and applying Vitapoint from a bottle, so that it would stay back from her forehead. Rachel preferred her hair the way it always had been, hiding much of her face. Ruth's hair was always neatly combed back and Rachel felt her father wanted her hair to be like her mother's.

Throughout her time in Coláiste Íde Rachel used to get a letter from Ruth every Friday, but she remembers only two from her father: Seán was ill on both occasions. On the first occasion a stool had fallen on his big toe and he was forced to stay at home, with one leg in the air. The other time she received a letter was when he had been involved in a car accident in 1971: his nose was badly injured and he was obliged to stay at home. She did, however, receive money from him by post on other occasions.

One of Rachel's fondest memories is a story told to her by her mother of the day Seán and Ruth started to go out together, while they were still students at UCC. Ruth remembered a white blanket of snow covering everything and few people to be seen outdoors. The pair had walked by themselves from the main College building, right down to the gates on the Western Road. They stopped and looked back. Their footprints were side by side in a long line stretching back the way they had come – the first steps of love in a blanket of snow.

this belongs better in the omitting section,
(Chapter 3)

Seán had always intended to teach his children music in a formal way and Ruth continually encouraged him to begin, but always got the same response – he was too busy at the moment but would do it soon. At first he was reluctant that they should go to any other teacher, but when Rachel went to Coláiste Íde, she was allowed to take lessons from the college's piano teacher. However, Seán often taught his children songs: Rachel remembers learning *Aililiú na Gamhna* and *An Seanduine* from him. She feels Seán's attitude to the piano was coloured by the pressure he had been put under when he was young.

Rachel reminisced about the fun they used to have going by car to Kenmare, where they would fish mackerel from the boat. Though not a good swimmer, Rachel went swimming one day. She coaxed Seán to go in as well, although he was always afraid of the water, having been thrown in unexpectedly when young. Notwithstanding the fact that he was wearing his life-jacket, a sudden fear gripped Seán and he held onto his daughter, who became extremely frightened, until Ruth came and saved them both.

Seán was extremely superstitious: Rachel said he would not pass her on the stair: she would have to remain at the bottom, if he were coming down, or else he would wait at the top for her to ascend. He

153

often spoke to her about death. When Ruth's father was staying with them in Cúil Aodha once, he became ill and all feared he was dying. 'Not a bit of it,' said Seán, 'that man will bury me yet.' Ruth was angry he should say such a thing. As it happened, Seán was wrong, since Ruth's father died a few months before him.

The local priest, Father Donncha Ó Conchúir, felt Seán had a strong religious faith and that his pose of being a non-believer, an agnostic, was for the benefit of his Dublin friends. He admitted that Ó Riada believed as strongly in various superstitions – as did his father and mother before him. Seán was always careful to ensure the appropriate person be the first to enter the house after midnight on New Year's Eve, otherwise they would not have luck. One year it happened that his son Eoin, who could be considered almost a redhead, was the first to cross the threshold and got a clout on the ear from his father for this transgression.

Peadar remembers his father crying when Tadhg Ó Mulláin died. Rachel spoke of Seán crying on another occasion, as he played the piano. As far as she can remember, it was in some way connected with the Northern troubles. Seán had made all the other children leave the room and was angry that Rachel had remained to see and hear him crying. Ó Riada played *Seán Ó Duibhir a' Ghleanna* at Tadhg's funeral. It was at Séamus Ó Muineacháin's funeral that *Gile Mear* was played for the first time on such a sad occasion. It was subsequently used as a recessional at the funerals of Seán himself, Ruth and the singer Diarmuid Ó Súilleabháin.

It is interesting to speculate how the ordinary people of Cúil Aodha viewed the famous stranger who had come into their midst. Dónal Ó Liatháin, a local schoolteacher, has said, 'Seán did not come furtively, but with a big splash and, as the song says, with the sound of trumpets.' Everyone wondered at this man, familiar with ministers of government and even the President of the State. Seán's neighbours were aware that a certain government minister had come to the house early one morning and was throwing stones at the upstairs window to waken Ó Riada, all the time shouting at the top of his voice: 'get up out of that, you lazy bastard, and come down here until I talk to you!' The locals also knew that Seán wanted to get his influential friends to work towards his own version of a cultural and economic revolution in Cúil Aodha.

The local people were proud of him because he presented their music and stories on radio and television. They would sometimes hear and see the storyteller, Éamonn Kelly, whom they knew well, starring in Seán's programmes. As time went on, more of them got to know him when he'd come seeking knowledge of the place and of themselves. In the process, they discovered some of them were related to him – the Ó Súilleabháins, for example, on his mother's side. Dónal remembers Seán coming to him one day to check if they might be related, as Julia Creedon was from the Kilnamartyra area, where Dónal's father, Niallais Ó Liatháin had been, for years, the local postman.

Ó Riada was familiar with the group from Cúil Aodha who would attend the Oireachtas in Dublin, where Cúil Aodha competitors were well-known for a long time as prizewinners in the various competitions. Among such were Seán Eoin a' Bháb, Diarmuid Ó Ríordáin, Páidí Thaidhg Pheig, Seán Ó Duinnín and many more.

It was through his choir, Cór Cúil Aodha, that many of them got to know Seán. That contact was friendly and without rancour, unlike his encounter with the local Court of Poetry, Dámhscoil Mhúscraí, that met at the beginning of every year, so that poets, mainly local, could discuss in verse the theme which had already been proposed by the secretary. Ó Riada wanted to bring the workings of the the court into the twentieth century and liven it up a bit, so that it would be suitable for television presentation. He could have attained his object in a less aggressive manner had he gone through the long-accepted channels of the president of the court, *An Suibhneach Meann* and the secretary,

Peadar Ó Liatháin. Bringing RTE in on the occasion was easy for Ó Riada, as he had plenty of friends in that organisation.

By the time the Court met that year, the hall was packed, which was unusual. RTE cameras were there and many outsiders had crowded in so some of the local poets could not find a place to sit. Seán had planned to intersperse the poetry with songs and the president was highly annoyed at this new development. He shouted at Seán to stop his carry-on and Ó Riada was heard telling him to be gone out of it. Seán's response to the whole affair was not untypical: after that night's happenings, he never again bothered with the annual court of poetry. As far as he was concerned, it had had its chance.

Poor Dónal Ó Liatháin was in somewhat of a quandary after the affair, as he was not only a member of Seán's choir, but the president of the Court was his uncle and his former teacher at primary school. Neither faction in the dispute felt it could completely trust Dónal, as he had connections on both sides, whereas Dónal himself felt that he was the only one who could see both sides of the story!

When a man decided to build a piggery near the Ó Riada's home, some felt it was being done on purpose to rile Seán, who, of course, opposed it vigorously, making the point that it would ruin the environment, as they had no proper way of disposing of the effluent. Seán lost the battle eventually and the piggery was built. Unfortunately, it soon became obvious that Ó Riada had been right.

Not all of Dónal's memories of the Ó Riada era in Cúil Aodha are of strife. The choir's first visit to the South Chapel in Cork was memorable: after the mass a woman came to them and said: 'why can't we have a choir like this every Sunday?' Such comment inspired them.

Dónal often drank with Ó Riada, but never saw him drunk, though he was drinking a lot towards the end. Dónal felt Cúil Aodha was not a suitable place for a person who might be inclined towards a drink problem. It was all right for the locals, as they only went on occasional sprees for special occasions and, while they could certainly drink a lot on the night, would then leave it until the next time. However, Seán had so many friends in so many places that he could frequently be drinking heavily.

Many of the locals noticed Ó Riada did not look well, on his return from his Canadian tour in 1971 and they were worried about him. One woman spoke to Ruth and Rachel on the matter, telling them to look after him. Some time earlier, Dónal Ó Mathúna, who had been at school in Farranferris with Seán, was having his car repaired in a Macroom garage and met Seán there. When Ó Riada left, the owner said to Dónal, 'Who was that old man you were talking to?' Dónal replied, 'That's no old man – he's only my own age, 38.'

Ó Mathúna spoke of Seán's school days. 'There's no doubt,' he said, 'that Ó Riada turned out to be the cleverest person in the whole school, but we were not aware of that. Music was not in any way important in the school in our time. Hurling was number one and, strangely enough,' he remarked, 'there was no science taught in the school until after the first atomic bomb fell on Hiroshima!'

CHAPTER 13

Ó R i a d a ' s   F i l m - m a k i n g

In the mid 1960s Seán set up a film company in Cúil Aodha, Draíon Films, primarily to make short films for some of the television shows in which he was involved, such as *Aililiú*. He employed Seán Ó Cíomháin, an old friend from Kerry, to be his assistant/secretary and coaxed Ronnie McShane from the Abbey Theatre to be his film-man. At first, Ronnie was part-time, but later operated on a full-time basis.

Roy Hammond, an English cameraman who had lived in Cork for many years, would come to Cúil Aodha once a week to work with Seán on the *Aililiú* television programme. They often drank together, either before their work or afterwards and Roy had a habit of going out to the Ó Riada's every Saturday night, when they would have plenty of drink, music and dancing, as well as liberal doses of poteen. Roy remembered a priest playing the whistle, Ronnie keeping the rhythm on spoons and the house full of music, song and dance till daybreak. Roy pointed out that this all happened in the days before Gardaí would be lying in wait for you. He remembered drinking in the pub with Seán once in November, when one of the locals began to mock him because he was wearing a poppy. Seán was quick to jump to his friend's defence, telling the mocker sharply that Roy had a right to wear any emblem he wished.

Seán and Roy were involved at one time in making short sections of film that would last for approximately seven minutes, for insertion into *Aililiú*, perhaps while Ceoltóirí Cualann or a solo fiddler, such as Denis Murphy, 'The Weaver', would be playing. RTE purchased the films from Ó Riada under contract. Roy has clear memories of one film they made, in which one of Seán's sons was kicking a young screaming pig on the backside, keeping time to the music. Éamonn de Buitléar warned Seán that if he allowed the film to be shown, Éamonn would resign from Ceoltóirí Cualann, which was, of course, the band playing the jig, *Gander in the Pratie Hole*, to accompany the kicking. Ó Riada insisted that he would show it and that it was none of Éamonn's business. The film was shown and no one resigned, though there was a certain public outcry about cruelty to animals.

They made another short film entitled *The Rocky Road to Dublin*, which showed Ronnie dressed as a tramp, trudging along the Lower Glanmire road, with a signpost for Dublin clearly on view behind him. There were more shots of Ronnie in Patrick Street and in the Chateau bar, where the landlady was at first happy that her bar should appear on Irish television. She was anything but satisfied, however, when Ronnie, rather over-acting his part, knocked over a glass of whiskey and slumped, very convincingly, onto the floor, in full camera-shot! She ejected them straight away, as she did not want to be seen on television, serving drink to a drunken beggar in her high class establishment.

At another time, Ó Riada himself was the camera-man, wearing dark glasses and discreetly taking shots of Ronnie from the back seat of a car, as he walked along the road and also getting nature-shots as fillers for *Aililiú*. It is surprising that Ó Riada had no television set (nor radio). Ronnie had to bring back a set from Dublin so they could see the results of their filming on *Aililiú*.

Ó Riada intended to do much more than short films for his television series. He had planned a long film on an Irish theme for the

American market but, by this time, colour television was becoming well established, which put paid to Seán's grand scheme, as he had only black and white equipment in Cúil Aodha. Much of the film already shot had to be thrown into the bin and with it, another Ó Riada dream.

Ronnie remembered the time Seán decided they would have to have a crane for the camera, as every real studio had one. Ronnie drew up plans, at Ó Riada's request, and they brought them to a blacksmith in Cork who devised (or improvised!) a 20 ft long crane within a fortnight, which was then parked in the front garden. The device had wheels but it was impossible to manoeuvre it on the roads of Cúil Aodha. Ó Riada, with his light-meter around his neck and wearing the obligatory dark glasses, was nearly killed in some of the early unsuccessful experiments. For a while, they had lead weights on loan from the Abbey Theatre, in an attempt to find the correct balance and when everything was right, Ronnie had to manipulate the crane from the rear, to ensure they had the correct angles for viewing whatever was to appear on screen.

In one film, Ronnie and Martin Fay were playing the parts of soldiers in a war. Ronnie had borrowed uniforms and rifles from old friends in the Army. The two actors had to dig trenches and man them, as soldiers would. When Seán called Ronnie, he had to desert his soldierly duties, jump up out of the trench and as soon as Seán shouted, 'Take one, Draíon Films', Ronnie would shut the clapper board with a bang and jump back into soldierly mode in the trench. At the end of the day's shooting all would retire to the studio – in other words, to Seán's room – to edit the material. Director Ó Riada, wearing cowboy boots he had got in America and puffing a cigar, certainly looked the part!

Éamonn de Buitléar says that Seán never believed in starting his projects at a low level. As he used to say to Ruth, 'If a thing is worth doing, it is worth doing well. If you are not going to do something right, don't do it at all'. He had collected books on filming in Hollywood and had, as usual, decided to go for the best. He bought, or hired, a Bell and Howell camera and used Roy as his camera man, until he decided he would do the job himself. Éamonn remembered one project that Ó Riada was serious about: he planned to buy 10,000 ft of archive film about the Battle of the Somme and interlace it with some of his own material, as well as writing his own script. He intended to film an opera but that was just another dream which did not materialise.

After a few years of this film work, Draíon Films ran out of cash and could not pay its staff, so Ó Riada had to let Ronnie and Seán Ó Cíomháin go. Seán went back to Kerry and Ronnie found work in a London hotel.

CHAPTER 14

D E A T H   O F   Ó   R I A D A

Seán was in the Bon Secours Hospital in Cork in the summer of 1971. He had been warned by doctors, after a previous time in hospital, that unless he gave up drink immediately he would have less than two years to live. He did manage to give it up for a time, but the damage had been done over a long period. Many who knew Seán at this time felt he wanted to be finished with life.

Seán Ó Sé remembers going out to Cúil Aodha and finding John Kelly, the fiddler, there with Seán. They were listening to an old tape of Ceoltóirí Cualann. It was clear that Seán was elated by the music but sad in himself. He looked across at John and said, 'Those were the good days, John.' 'And they'll come back again, Seán,' was Kelly's answer, in an attempt to cheer him up. 'I'm afraid not,' Ó Riada said. 'Believe me John – they will not.'

Ó Riada's sister, Louise, remembers the awful shock she got when Father James Good rang her from the Bon Secours Hospital to tell her that Seán was there, and how Father Donncha Ó Conchúir had given him the last rites. Although Louise, Walter and the family had just arrived in Limerick from a visit to the Connemara Gaeltacht, they drove straight to Cork, but were not allowed into Seán's room, in case they would disturb him. They went to the parents' home in Dorgan's road and spent the night there. At breakfast next morning, Seán's father was repeatedly saying, 'God's will be done'. This maddened Louise, as she felt their will should be done, so that Seán would not die.

One doctor said Seán had cancer and there was no hope. They were advised to look for a second opinion, at which stage Garech de Brúin of Claddagh Records, who had recently recorded Seán's last performance on harpsichord, was drawn into their discussions. Seán Ó Sé remembers Ruth and Garech being in his house one day when Garech rang a consultant in Vienna, to see if he would come to Cork to operate on Seán, but nothing came of it. Then Ruth asked Garech to contact King's College Hospital in London, using his friend Lady Cowley's father as an intermediary, to see if Seán could go under the care of a famous liver consultant. That was arranged but it was then discovered that all flights to London were full. Garech rang Tim O'Driscoll, head of Aer Lingus and he arranged a flight for Seán from Cork to London, on a plane that had been diverted to pick him up.

Seán Ó Sé was in Cork airport on 14 September to say goodbye to Ó Riada, but discovered that there was a serious problem: the company that had brought Ó Riada there in a private ambulance were not prepared to let their stretcher go to London, in case they would not get it back. Ó Riada lay in the ambulance and a young doctor was inserting a drip that had malfunctioned, into his wrist. Seán Ó Sé spoke to Ó Riada and remembers thinking that Ó Riada somehow reminded him of a rabbit, caught in a trap that could not escape. He was in full possession of his senses, as he looked at them and at the drip going into his arm.

Seán Ó Sé rang his friend John O'Shea, who worked for the Cork Fire Brigade, looking for help. Richie Walsh, who was in charge of the station where John worked, arranged that a stretcher would be sent out immediately, and the problem was solved. Seán bade goodbye to Ó Riada and said he'd see him soon but, in answering, Ó Riada let him know he did not think they would meet again.

There was more trouble in London. The stretcher was too big for the hospital lift and Seán had to be brought up the fire escape outside the building. There was a further half-hour wait outside the door of his room, while they looked for a key to open it.

Louise phoned the hospital twice that night to check that everything was all right. She was put through directly to Seán's room and he told her a long story about a drug ring in the hospital. He said he had heard doctors and nurses discussing it but that he had pretended to be asleep, as he knew they would kill him if they thought he knew about the drugs. Louise told him not to worry and that she would come to London next day with Walter. 'It will be too late then, Louise', was his answer. Louise kept talking to him until he settled down and then said goodbye. She had succeeded in quietening her brother, but she herself was now sick with worry. Walter was at a meeting and she could not contact him, so she rang Father James Good, who was staying in Limerick with the Redemptorists. He advised herself and Walter to fly to London next day and rang her later that night, having booked two seats to London for them on the first flight of the day. When he discovered she did not have much money, he gave her £100 in cash and a cheque for another £100 that she could cash with a friend of his in the Irish Centre in London. He then drove them to Shannon, where they caught the early plane to London.

During the first couple of days in the hospital, Louise was almost continuously at her brother's bedside, as he was still frightened about the danger he was in from the doctors and nurses. Even when the nurses were assisting him medically, they encouraged Louise to keep talking to Seán from outside the screens, so that he would know she was still there and might not feel so worried.

Each night they were in London, Ruth, Walter, Tom Kinsella and Louise would have a meal in the hospital, before paying their last visit to Seán, about a quarter of an hour before midnight. He wanted them to be there at that time because he felt that whatever was going to happen would happen at midnight and if midnight passed without anything untoward occurring, he would be safe for another day. He would tell them to go away at a quarter-past twelve and he could calmly rest.

Peadar and Father Donncha Ó Conchúir were next to arrive from Cúil Aodha. Louise and Walter decided to go back to Limerick for a time. Louise remembers their parting and Seán thanking her for coming over to him. 'You are very welcome,' she replied. 'Give me a call if you need help.' 'And I'll always be there,' said Seán, 'if you need me.'

Len Clifford and Garech de Brúin were there around the same time. Garech was on his way to Antibes to visit his mother. Seán told him one day that he thought he was dying, but at other times he'd be in good form and singing away. Seán received a welcome letter in Irish from Bishop Caird, and Bishop Éamonn Casey called in en route to Rome, and gave him the last rites.

Éamonn de Buitléar remembered getting a call from Ruth, just after he returned from visiting Seán in London. She wanted Éamonn to come back immediately, as Seán had taken a bad turn. She emphasised the seriousness of it by letting him know there would be a taxi waiting to bring him directly to the hospital. As it happened, Éamonn did not meet the taxi, so took another cab. Some time later, the first taximan came to the hospital, asking in a strong Cockney accent, 'I'm looking for Mr Riadah's butler. Is 'e' 'ere?'

Éamonn admits he was frightened on seeing Seán so weak. He gave him a shave, the last one Ó Riada was to have and spoke to an Irish nurse. She told him there was no hope for Seán and she had seen many Irish in the last few years coming in with the same disease, cirrhosis of the liver, with nothing ahead of them but death.

There was another emergency when the doctors announced Seán would have to undergo an operation, with little hope of success: they said it was nine to one against survival. 'Well,' said Seán, 'if there is even a ten to one chance, I'll take take it and have the operation.' Afterwards he was put into intensive care and only Ruth was allowed to see him – for a short time each day. Louise and Walter had by this time returned to London and Louise was allowed to see him once. She remembers he had tubes going into every part of his body and an oxygen mask covered his face. She was told not to speak, in case she would disturb him. The doctors were surprised Seán was interested in all they were doing and had already asked for pen and paper so that he could write them notes about his condition and the care he was receiving.

Three days later he was shifted back to his own room on the upper floor and things were going well, until he had a heart attack on the Thursday. There was an explosion of excitement in the hospital, with alarm bells, doctors and nurses running everywhere – no time for talk – just action. The patient was wheeled back quickly to intensive care, only to find that the bed was too wide and defied the staff's best efforts to manoeuvre it into the intensive care unit. Eventually, the panic was over. The usual phone calls were made to Ireland, telling their friends to stop worrying, as things were all right once more. It began to seem, throughout the week, that each phone call was a denial of the last one – alternate messages of hope and despair.

Seán had a second heart attack on that Saturday, which greatly weakened him. The doctors were adamant he could not survive a third one. Éamonn de Buitléar phoned Ronnie McShane, who was working in London, to tell him that Ó Riada was in King's College Hospital – dying. It was the first direct news of Seán that Ronnie had received since leaving Ireland and he was deeply shocked.

He went straight there and met Éamonn and Ruth, who put her arms around him and began to cry. She told him to go to see Seán. The television in his room was showing Star Trek, with the volume turned up: Ronnie saw a weak old man in the bed, whom he did not recognise, propped up by pillows. Ronnie could not believe this old man was his friend. The patient turned his head and saw the visitor.

'Ronnie,' he said. For the first time in his life, Ronnie saw tears in Ó Riada's eyes. He grasped Seán's hand without speaking: there was nothing to be said. They kept looking at each other for a long time, before Ronnie went away.

Ruth was completely worn out and had been given a pill on the Saturday, so that she could get a much-needed sleep in the hospital's rest room. Later that night, Walter went downstairs to phone Ireland, with strict instructions from Louise to let everyone at home know that the danger was not past, particularly after the second heart attack.

Louise was waiting in the upstairs room when news came from the intensive care unit that Seán had died. It was about 11 o'clock at night. The two nurses who told her said she should stay in the room until the doctors came, to give her the news officially. 'I can't stay here,' Louise said, 'I must find my husband.' She ran downstairs but Walter was not to be found. She was so confused she asked every stranger she met if they had seen him, telling everyone that her brother had just died. Then she saw Walter coming towards her, with a look of satisfaction on his face. 'I've just been into the chapel,' he said, 'and I'm very, very happy. Seán is going to be all right – no doubt about it.' Louise replied, 'He's at peace at last. He passed away a short time ago.'

The question then arose – what should they do about Ruth? Should they waken her or let her sleep, since there was nothing to be done now. They decided at last to awaken her with the bad news. 'I know,' was her immediate reply. She bowed her head and said, 'Just think of that – he came in here a while ago, in through that door there, and I sent him away.' They all stayed silent for a long time.

The nurses told them they ought to remain in the hospital. Beds were made up for them in private rooms, with the proviso that they had to leave before seven o'clock in the morning, when the day staff would be coming on duty, since they had not received official permission for what they were doing.

Next day, the pressure of all that had to be done urgently began, both in England and Ireland. They were able to contact Seán Ó Sé in Cork early next morning, asking him to convey the news to Seán's parents before they would hear it on a radio bulletin. The parents did not have a phone, so Seán Ó Sé kept them in touch with their son's condition in London. Seán Mac Réamoinn arrived at the hospital that day, as he had heard the news on radio as he was passing through London.

There was a suggestion in the hospital that they might do a post-mortem examination, as was normal for a sudden death, so the body would not be released for some time, thus delaying the funeral. The Irish embassy intervened on their behalf and permission was given to bring the body back to Ireland on Tuesday 5 October. However, Ruth was dissatisfied with the compromise that was made to allow Seán's removal from the hospital: they were forced to accept a certificate which named the cause of death as 'cirrhosis of the liver, caused by alcohol'. They were asked to officially identify Ó Riada's body and, since Walter was busy with other arrangements, it was Mac Réamoinn who went with Ruth and Louise for the formal identification.

Ruth, Louise and Walter accompanied Seán's coffin to Cork on an Aer Lingus flight. Ruth had asked Ronnie McShane to drive her from the hospital to Heathrow, though the Irish embassy had offered to bring her there.

When their plane reached Cork they found an enormous crowd waiting at the airport, including the Ó Riada children. Louise and Ruth were in the same car as Lia and Sorcha, the youngest of the children, as they drove to Cúil Aodha. Louise does not remember much of that day, except hearing the children talking in the back of the car. 'Do you think,' one asked the other, 'that it's really Seán inside that box?'

Louise's chief memory of those days is a feeling of empty nothing-ness, even when she saw people around her crying bitterly. That mood passed and she became angry with Seán, that he should leave them help-less. Then she became angry with God, who had permitted this to happen.

As soon as Seán Ó Sé got the news of Seán's death, he went straight to Seán's parents to tell them. He did not need to say the words. When Julia opened the door and saw him, she said, 'It's not good news that brings you here so early in the morning. He's dead.' The father had already gone to early mass in the Lough Church, where Seán collected him and brought him home. He too knew what had happened once he saw Seán Ó Sé approaching him in the church. Seán drove the pair out to Cúil Aodha later and he remembers the rosary being said continuously throughout the journey. He was with them on the day of the funeral and remembers they spent every spare moment in prayer.

As the body was taken to Cúil Aodha, hundreds of cars followed the procession through Coachford, Macroom and Ballyvourney, and crowds lined the roads all the way. Shops were shut in his honour and children stood outside every school. The late Professor Fleischmann remarked that it resembled a king coming back among his own people. Father Donncha Ó Conchúir received the coffin at the church in Cúil Aodha that evening.

The sculptor, Séamus Murphy from Cork, was asked to make an impression for Ó Riada's death-mask. He asked me to come to the church in Cúil Aodha later that night when everyone had gone. The undertaker opened the coffin and locked the two of us into the church, promising to return later. I spent a couple of hours helping Séamus with the death-mask until the undertaker returned to the lonely church to close the coffin. As he let down the lid, I stooped lower to have the very last, very sad view of Seán.

The church in Cúil Aodha was full next day for the funeral mass at one o'clock. Father Donncha Ó Conchúir was the celebrant, in the presence of Bishop Aherne. Amplifiers allowed the huge crowd outside the church to follow the proceedings. There was music from Willie Clancy, Tony McMahon, Ceoltóirí Cualann and Cór Cúil Aodha, with Peadar Ó Riada on the organ.

After mass, piper Alf Kennedy led the funeral procession to St Gobnait's cemetery. There were two people following the funeral whom Seán would have been particularly glad to see there – Charles J. Haughey and General Tom Barry.

This graveside group at the burial of Seán Ó Riada shows his widow, Ruth, linked to her son, Peadar, together with the other Ó Riada children, Seán's mother Julia and sister Louise Verling. On Peadar's left are Seán's cousins from Clare. Standing a little to Ruth's right is Éamon de Buitléar.

Seán's parents had accepted their son's death with great fortitude, but when the coffin was being let down into the grave, Julia shuddered and later said to Seán Ó Sé, who was with her, that she knew now there was no suffering worse than the death of one of your own family. John Kelly, fiddle player with Ceoltóirí Cualann, came up to them both and simply said, 'He lifted us all up.'

CHAPTER 15

W H I C H   S E Á N   Ó   R I A D A ?

Seán Ó Riada had so much talent that different people saw different Seáns. He was, of course, a gifted musician who played both piano and violin, could appreciate and perform anything from traditional Irish to jazz and classical music and was involved with modern developments in more serious European music. He was a writer and talented journalist who worked on radio, television and musical drama. When resident in Kerry, he lived by his writing and was published regularly in *The Irish Times.* He was a film-director and formed his own film company. Above all else, he was a composer of the first rank, something which is becoming more obvious as time goes on.

Seán made a point of showing whatever side of his character he wished, depending on the company and the context. He always had something of the chameleon about him. It was almost an involuntary reaction, but it was always in his own control.

I have seen a notebook of his, dated January 1948. On the flyleaf he penned the following modest description of himself: 'Genius; Authority on Literature, Art and Music.' He was just sixteen years of age!

Even those who spent a lot of time in his company admitted they did not really know the full Seán – and felt they never would. Everyone knew whatever Ó Riada was prepared to show them. So it turned out that no one really knew the complete Seán – not even his wife.

Who was the Seán Ó Riada I knew? I first met him in 1963 at a celebration in the Vienna Woods Hotel in Glanmire, organised by Prof. Fleischmann, on the retirement of Seán Neeson from his post as Cork Corporation Lecturer in Irish music. We presented a clavichord to Seán Neeson and when the meal was finished Ó Riada played Carolan's Concerto on the instrument. Ó Riada had accepted the newly-created post of lecturer in Irish music and we were all extremely happy about that, as his name was held in high esteem.

I remember discussing with him the problems associated with raising an Irish-speaking family, which both of us were doing. He said we should be in touch and various visits to the Ó Riada home in Cúil Aodha ensued. Ruth and he had five children at that time – Peadar, Rachel, Eoin, Alastair and Cathal; two more were to be born in Cúil Aodha – Sorcha, and Liadh.

We discussed the radio programmes he had presented before then and, in particular, the intense dislike he seemed to have of accordions. I was an accordionist myself and had played for years in ceilí bands in Liverpool and regarded the instrument highly. Seán just laughed and said one had to go a bit overboard to make one's point in an argument.

Only for Seán, I might not be playing pipes now, as he was the one who advised me to take them up and encouraged me to persist with them, as a means of getting to the soul of the music. Although I had a long acquaintance with the music before I met Seán, I did get a new view of it when I eventually began to attend his Bachelor of Music degree lectures in the late 1960s.

From 1968 until he died in 1971, I attended Seán's lectures. He took classes in three subjects: history of music, Irish music, and keyboard harmony. He had a keen musical ear and perfect pitch. From the back of the room, in our keyboard harmony class, he would name every note and even which finger was on each key.

He had a good sense of humour. Our textbook was *Man and his Music*. Seán based his lecture on a new chapter each week and I thought I had him in a slight pickle when I showed him who the pre-Baroque composers for that day were – Schütz, Scheidt and Schein. I told him I was looking forward to hearing him announce the names before a class that included a clerical student and a Christian Brother. We laughed at the prospect but the last laugh was on me. Seán came in to begin his lecture and said, 'Today we'll study the pre-Baroque composers. Tomás has something to say about them. Tell us first, Tomás, what are the names of these three important composers?' The class knew Seán had caught me in my own trap.

On the first Sunday in October 1971 – a day I shall never forget – when Matt Cranitch, Tom Barry and myself, as the group Na Filí, were practising in our front room, my neighbour came to the window and said: '*Tá an Riadach caillte*' (Ó Riada is dead). Séamus had just heard the news on his car radio.

Within the week, I had started to give the Irish music lectures in the Music Department.

There were fine students in that first degree class – Eilís Cranitch, who was joint editor with myself of Seán's second mass *Aifreann 2*, Nóirín Ní Riain, who has done so much in Irish liturgical music, Cathal Dunne, who sang for Ireland in Eurovision, Seán Fitzpatrick, who later headed the Cork International Choral Festival and Mícheál Ó Súilleabháin, who continued the lectures in Irish music when I resigned in 1975. Mícheál has since made a considerable name for himself as a professor in the University of Limerick.

Ó Riada was the only genius I have ever encountered. While genius certainly implies high intellect, Seán also had the ability to draw others towards him by the sheer force of his personality and impel them towards a level of consciousness of which they would hardly have been aware previously. Ó Riada's genius will be seen in the way he interacted with and influenced his own world, in the the way he attracted and held the attention of the people of Ireland as no contemporary had done, in his truly artistic view of every aspect of cultural life: in short, the intangible spirit that has gone with him into the grave in St Gobnait's cemetery, where he lies with Ruth, his first and only true love. 'The three finest things in this world,' he once said, after returning from a musical sojourn abroad, 'are your wife, your children and coming home safely to them'.

Some time after Seán's death, as a mild rebuke to the poetic fraternity, I wrote this rather sardonic poem:

SEÁN Ó RIADA
Jostling poets parse the bones of a dead nightingale
Condoning the stiff-spread wing:
Measure him for a verse
Now he can no longer sing.

Important questions must be posed again: who was the real Seán, where was he to be found, and what were the things in which he really believed? Before one can answer these questions, one must ask an even more fundamental one: can we accept Ó Riada's own word in these matters?

For Ó Riada, fantasy was important and a necessary part of life. Even as a student at University, his friends remember him telling stories that could not have been true, for example, how cruel his father had been, beating him unmercifully and beating him often. It is fairly clear that many of the stories of his adventures in France in 1955 were pure fantasy. Ó Riada himself often referred to the creature of fantasy that resided within his own mind. Bellingham was one of the names he used in referring to him and he ascribed many opinions to poor Bellingham.

Seán O Sé and Seán Ó Riada, who were good friends, came from similar backgrounds: both had parents who were public servants – Ó

Sé's father a teacher and Ó Riada's a Garda. Ó Sé felt such children were a little isolated amongst their fellows, both at school and at play, as certain things might not be said to them, in case they would be passed on to their parents. He made the point that in his own case and probably in Ó Riada's, this resulted in an innate shyness and a tendency to live in a rather separate fantasy world.

Another friend of Ó Riada, the film-maker Louis Marcus, remembers what Ó Riada said when he was having some difficulty with the music for *An Tine Bheo*:

'This is the hardest job I have ever had to do – to try and bring a fresh mind to this subject – my mind was already overexposed to 1916 before I started. I know now what my hell will be.'

In *The Achievement of Seán Ó Riada*, Marcus touched on Ó Riada's fantasy world:

He had already experienced at least one other hell that I knew of. It started towards the end of 1961, when he was still living in Dublin, and lasted several months. No doubt there were personal problems involved, and the strain of trying to keep a large family on a few pounds a week didn't help either. But the crisis went much deeper than that. While he maintained something of his public ebullience, in private he was sometimes close to tears and, I feared, to losing his reason.

As usual with Seán, the manifestations were diverse and brilliant. One day in the Oval Bar, with only a pounds between the two of us to get drunk on, he was agonising about the limit he seemed to have reached with Irish music. (Only in his later liturgical music was he to make any further real advance.) Suddenly he began to tell me with manic glee his idea for a musical horror film to be called *The Killer Chord*.

The hero is a renowned composer who performs secret experiments on the lethal possibilities of music. Starting with the

175

known power of sound to smash a glass, he discovers increasingly ghastly potential for destruction. Finally, he devises a chord which, by its particular combination of pitches, harmonies, tone colour, volume and duration, should kill the listener.

His next work is announced with the startling news that the final chord will not be played in rehearsal and that the orchestral parts for it will be distributed only as the concert begins. Tension mounts as we see the work performed and observe not only the musicans and audience in the concert hall, but also the millions listening at home or on car radios. As the final moment approaches, the composer, who conducts the piece himself, stuffs his ears with impenetrable plugs. Then the fatal chord is played. The orchestra and audience collapse dead, people slump by their firesides all over the country and cars with radios slaughter hundreds as they career out of control. The composer, calmly removing his earplugs, has survived. I pointed out to Seán that such an event would decimate the cultured section of society and leave the rest virtually unscathed. He didn't seem to mind.

There were blacker moments still. Antonioni's film *L'Aventura* caused him the anguish that Resnais had a year before. 'It's about giving, about not being able to give any more. Either in your work or in your life, you've got to give. But,' he added ruefully, 'you can't do it in both.' For a few days he was obsessed with the idea of going to live in Rome. But that passed. He was very disturbed too by an ancient poem he had come across in Irish about a child locked in a prison cell, who knocks on the wall but receives no reply. He listened to music a lot at this time, music that seemed to have some urgent meaning for him. Edith Piaf: 'She's saying no, but she's saying it affirmatively.' And Mahler's *Das Lied von der Erde* in which the agony on the word *Ewig* always brought tears to his eyes.

Regarding Seán's French sojourn, it is true that he had already visited Paris in 1954 and had played two of his own compositions (subsequently withdrawn) on French radio in the series *Soloistes
Internationaux*. On his much publicised visit there in 1955, after his
sudden departure from his employment as Assistant Music Director
with Radio Éireann (which some viewed as an escape from his responsibilities) Seán is said to have formed friendships with the Scots composer Ian Hamilton and to have been in contact with the composer
Messiaen and Schmitt. He claimed to have been offered the post of
conductor with an orchestra in Saigon, but turned it down because at
that time Saigon was a war zone. He also claimed to have accompanied
the singer Juliette Greco. He described his efforts to make money by
selling pictures on the streets of Paris, without success.

Many of Ó Riada's fantasies were connected with sexual matters
and included wild meetings with wonderful women. Whether they
were true or false, Seán was able to tell, or invent, details of their pas-
sionate love. Sculptor Eddie Delaney told me one such story he had
heard from Seán about a night in Garech de Brúin's house. It concerned a certain naked female who had appeared from behind a bush
at the bottom of the garden and of subsequent wonders. Years later,
Eddie was asked to do a picture for the cover of the score of *Nomos 1*,
when Woodtown were publishing it. He drew a picture of Seán's
naked lady in the bush. When Ó Riada saw it he was not pleased. 'In
the name of God,' he said, 'why did you put that awful thing on the
front of *Nomos 1*? What connection can that have with either myself
or the music?' He had already forgotten his fantasy.

Ó Riada sometimes could not, or did not, differentiate between
truth and fantasy, between the world as it was and the world as he
would wish it to be. Who is to say that such continual composition is
not a part of the armoury of a composer?

There are those who say that Seán Ó Riada was the most significant artist to remain in Ireland in the post-Second World War period

– and that includes writers and painters. He certainly touched the ordinary people in a special way. This was surprising, as many pundits would have said that music in Ireland was perhaps the poorest of the arts, lacking artistic status, as a result of our isolation from the wellspring of European classical music.

Whatever about our classical roots, no one doubts that the native tradition of music here is a fundamental component of everything that we Irish are. It is generally admitted now, though it might not have been acknowledged when he was alive, that Ó Riada made a very significant contribution to an understanding of and appreciation of what was really important in our native traditions. Without him, it is certain there would have been no upsurge of popularity and acclaim for traditional music, such as has occurred since his death. His serious European music (for want of a better title) is hugely appreciated by many, while others claim that an Irish composer such as Seán, with no genuine tradition of classical music behind him, had no hope of making a significant contribution in this sphere.

But Ó Riada was not a normal Irishman. This was clear from his manner of dress, even when he had no money, as well as from his unique presence in company. It was most apparent in his intellectual and artistic contact with his professional colleagues.

Seán Ó Mórdha, maker of the very important television documentary on Seán, *The Blue Note*, was in no doubt that Ó Riada had made a significant contribution to traditional music. 'Neither the musicians who were there in his time nor the groups, such as Planxty, Chieftains, Mícheál Ó Súilleabháin, De Danann, etc., could compare with Seán. Most of them, of course, are excellent musicians – able to do clever and pretty things with well-worn themes, but Ó Riada had an unusual imagination – something those others don't possess. He made fundamental changes in the whole system and gave Irish music a position and status it never had before his time.'

Around 1966 some of RTE's television producers refused to have any further dealings with Ó Riada, claiming they were tired of his working methods. That was when Seán came back to Dublin to meet Rugheimer, the Swedish head of television programmes. Ó Riada walked into Rugheimer's office without an appointment and they spent more than an hour in discussion although the Head of Television Programmes had said he could not spare Seán five minutes. Rugheimer was excited by their meeting and exclaimed, 'Why haven't I met this Ó Riada before now?!' Unlike the television producers, their boss did not see a problem working with Seán and Ó Riada resumed his duties on television.

Some Dublin people were critical of Seán's move to Cúil Aodha, from an artistic point of view, as he left behind him everything that was important for his artistic life. Many felt his film-making in Cúil Aodha was simply a sporting diversion and he was not taking himself seriously as a composer, in this final period of his life. They felt it was a rather adolescent attempt to be more Irish than the Irish.

Seán had a special room set aside in his home as a work-room and some Dublin acquaintances regarded it as just a secret place where he could spend hours by himself, reading novels and science fiction, but not doing any worthwhile work on his own music. They felt Seán was not committed to his University work in Cork, which occupied a mere few hours a week, without any serious responsibilities.

Seán Ó Mórdha told of a meeting held in Dublin's Hibernian Hotel in 1961, between playwright Brian Friel and Ó Riada, about an opera which Tyrone Guthrie intended to stage. Seán was to provide the music and he seemed genuinely excited at the prospect. However, nothing was heard subsequently from Seán, as nothing was heard on other projects from which he walked away.

Some of his critics deny Seán's greatness as a composer, though they will admit that he was an extremely good arranger for orchestra, without having much creativity of his own. Even those who have a considerable regard for his work would say his best work was done in

Dublin and he did nothing significant during the five years of his life in Cúil Aodha. However, those of that opinion must be ignorant of the liturgical music he composed there.

Others would say Ó Riada could have been a great composer of songs, in the style of Hölderlin, had he been satisfied to work at his art. Equally, they felt he could have done well setting poetry – that of Auden, for example, or the Irish poet, Seán Ó Ríordáin.

On 28 March 1971, the *Sunday Press* carried an article on Seán. It showed a photograph of Seán carrying his gun, on a shooting expedition and the caption was 'A New Irish Opera: Ó Riada has sketch ready'. The final paragraph reads, 'If he has any ambition it is "to live until I am 500 years old". In Cúil Aodha, of course, because "it is the only place in the world to live".'

Looking at Ó Riada's life, it is clear that this multi-talented man produced a significant corpus of music that will survive and increase his reputation in the future. He gave the Irish people a new vision of the beauty and excellence of their native music. He was, by any standard, an intellectual of the first rank, who remained true to his personal vision of the integration of art and life.

APPENDIX I

Ó RIADA AND ACTON

In 1970 Seán Ó Riada performed in University College Dublin at a concert, after which *The Irish Times* critic Charles Acton wrote of his 'Mendelssohnian harmony' applied to Irish music – a comment which hurt Ó Riada and caused him to play the pieces from that concert for our B. Mus. class, to show that Acton was wrong.

Ó Riada gave a solo performance in Liberty Hall, Dublin on Bastille Day, 14 July 1971, which was reviewed in *The Irish Times* on 15 July by Acton. It was Ó Riada's last public performance before going into hospital in August. Acton's severe criticism led to a response in the paper from Ó Riada and to a further letter from Acton in *The Irish Times*.

The correspondence is reproduced below with an incomplete draft of a final reply from Seán, which was never published. The Ó Riada-Acton duel also brought comment from other readers, as shown. The final sad word belonged to Acton, when he wrote Seán's obituary in October of that year.

Seán Ó Riada One-Man Show Lacked Polish

Charles Acton

Seán Ó Riada gave what was called a one-man show in Liberty Hall, Dublin, last night, using a harpsichord and a piano.

Just after his opening, Mr Ó Riada introduced us to the tune, 'Father Halpin's Topcoat', and dressed it up as a modern French folk-song on the piano, as Mozart on the harpsichord (not that Mozart had much use for harpsichords), á la Russe, as Strauss (slightly Richard), as Beethoven, as bel canto, as Spanish, as Chopin – all in the tradition of Joseph Cooper, Alec Templeton, and dozens before them. I am afraid I found myself reflecting that here were styles falsified one after another, added to by the falsity of microphones in a hall that surely does not need them, and symbolised by the plastic flowers decorating the platform. Had Mr Ó Riada's stylistic impersonations been really slickly worked out and presented with true professional polish, one would recommend him to Maureen Potter as a Gael of Laughter. In fact, the actual standard was better suited to the private party or the reasonably lubricated cabaret.

Thence he ambled through a number of tunes in a gently entertaining or interesting way. He came close to being of absorbing interest in telling us about H. Martin Freeman's collection from Ballyvourney in 1913-1918 and how the then 37-year-old Peg O'Donoghue had sung an aisling exactly as she had sung it to Seán himself last year aged 94. But when he told us that he was playing it on the piano 'exactly as she sang it' and added thirds and sixths and various harmonies, I began to distrust his 'exactness'.

He entertained us by showing how a song titled 'Robin is my Delight, Ochone, Ochone' from Chappell's *Song Book* was 'God save the Queen' in spite of the '*Ochone*' – but Scholes's reference to Chappell is entitled 'Franklin is fled away'. Can we therefore trust his assertion that the archetypal 'Star-spangled Banner' was a tune called 'Anacreon' in London but originally by Carolan (1670-1738). More pedestrian scholarship asserts that the tune was that of 'Anacreon in Heaven' by John Stafford Smith (1750-1836).

Gently entertaining though the show was, it seemed to me to be neither professional enough for the variety stage nor of an adequate musical standard to detain a music critic beyond the first half. Seán Ó Riada's gifts remain enormous. Is this performance not selling himself too cheaply and indiscriminately in the market place? And is there not a word for that?

An Open Letter to Charles Acton
From his friend, Seán Ó Riada
My dear Charles,

As you know, and as many of my friends know, it is not my custom to write letters, either private or public. However, on August 1st, the Festival of Lughnasa, I shall be forty years of age: this approaching watershed has induced me to try to write one letter to yourself, in the hope that it will be both privately and publicly understood.

For some years now, you have been kind enough to take notice in *The Irish Times*, and elsewhere, of my musical activities. So kind, in fact, that I have come to think of you as a sort of well-meaning uncle, sometimes afraid that his black-sheep nephew might be about to stray, to fall into error, to do the wrong thing. In other words, you have tempered your praise with admonishment. Admonish, admonish – this is what one's favourite uncles do. Nephews, unfortunately, rarely live up to their uncle's expectations, nor obey satisfactorily their admonishings. And if an uncle may admonish, it is only Christian and charitable to allow a nephew his chance to admonish, in exchange.

As you know, Charles, I am a lecturer in the music department of University College Cork (as well, of course, as being a composer), a profession which is rather commonly described as 'academic' ... just as you yourself would, I suppose, be rather commonly described as a 'critic'. Now, 'academics' and 'critics' have one duty in common, an obligation to be faithful to the facts. The 'critic' may voice opinions, praise, or condemn, but the facts are of premier and paramount importance.

Your notice of my last concert, my 'one-man show', in Liberty Hall, on Bastille Day, 1971, gave a number of examples of your disregard for facts. You asserted that Mozart 'had not much use for harpsichords'. Hmm ... really, Charles? You quoted me as saying that Miss Peg O'Donoghue ('the then 37-year-old', referring to the years 1913-18!) sang an aisling to me last year at the age of 94. Tsk, tsk, Charles, you weren't listening properly, and a music critic should always listen. What I said was that Miss Gobnait Baróid, or, in English, Miss Abbey Barrett, who was described by A. Martin Freeman as being about 37 years of age in 1914 (see No. 23 of *The Journal of the Folksong Society*, published London, January, 1920) sang one of the songs – not an aisling – noted by Freeman from her in 1914, in exactly the same way for me last year. The point of that was to illustrate the consistency and importance of oral tradition. I then played on the piano a different song from the Freeman collection, noted by him from Miss Peg O'Donoghue, called *Aisling Gheal*. It would indeed have been miraculous had she sung it to me last year, as she was 78 in 1914. You took exception to my use of thirds and sixths and 'various harmonies' in my accompaniment of the melody. Now, I did not claim to play this tune on the piano 'exactly as she sang it' – I never heard her sing it; I just played the tune exactly as it occurs in the Freeman collection, with the addition of 'various harmonies' which have been used in this country and in the native Irish musical tradition for at least four centuries. If that seems too modern for you, Charles, perhaps you are being just a little puritanical? But more about harmony later.

Next, you said that I showed how a song called 'Robin is my Delight, Ochone, Ochone' from Chappell's *Song Book* was 'God Save the Queen'. I did not do that, Charles. I simply played the tune and let the audience and the critics draw their conclusions. Academics are rarely satisfied with secondary or tertiary sources of information, and, great as is my respect for Doctor Scholes, that tune does occur in Chappell (specifically, in '*The Ballad Literature and Popular Music of the Olden Time*' by William Chappell, Vol. 1 of the Dover edition, p.370) 'exactly' as I played it. You should read the note on p.369, and having done so, you may dig for the title 'Robin Is My Delight, O hone, O hone,' as I did.

You next said: 'Can we ... trust his assertion that the archetypal 'Star-spangled Banner' was ... originally by Carolan (1670-1738)? More pedestrian scholarship asserts that the tune was ... by John Stafford Smith (1750-1836)'. Pedestrian is the flattering word for this kind of scholarship, my dear Charles. If you have matriculated in the necessary subjects, and should you wish to apply, I am sure that University College Cork, would accept you as a student, and I would then enlighten you, as one of my students, on this matter.

I was amused to see how nimbly and nobly Doctor Donal O'Sullivan (for whom I have the greatest respect) sprang to your side in his letter to *The Irish Times* regarding this tune. I quote him: 'I would refer him (with, I hope, due modesty) to my two-volume *Carolan: The Life, Times, and Music of an Irish Harper*, published by Messrs, Routledge and Kegan Paul in 1958. It makes no mention of this tune, and the style shows that it could not possibly be one of his compositions. 'Doctor O'Sullivan's charming modesty is not misplaced. However, his two-volume work does not include another of Carolan's compositions, cherished under the title 'Athlone' by the Church of Ireland for nearly two centuries, the setting of the 60th psalm to Carolan's tune (see Weyman's 'Melodia Sacra'). And as for his judgment of what is, or is not Carolan's style, can we trust it when we consider his inclusion, as one of Carolan's tunes, of the aria 'O Lovely Peace' from *Judas Maccabaeus* by George Frederick Handel, no relation at all of Toirdhealbhach Ó Cearbhalláin (see No. 177 in Doctor O'Sullivan's two-volume work). Facts are, indeed, of the greatest importance to the 'critic' and 'academic' alike.

You ended your notice of my Bastille Day performance by saying: 'Seán Ó Riada's gifts remain enormous. Is this perfomance not selling himself too cheaply and indiscriminately in the market place? And is there not a word for that?'

The word which you implied, Charles, was 'prostitution'.

Would it have been prostitution had I given this kind of peformance for nothing? Or if I had sold myself a little more expensively, charged a higher fee? I have, on occasion, done this kind of thing for nothing. Perhaps you would regard that more as 'promiscuity' than 'prostitution'? Surely the essential element in prostitution is its dishonesty.

My concert advertisements never claimed that I was going to play Bach fugues, sing in the seán-nós style, or do four-part contrapuntal improvisations. I can and will, of course, produce four-part improvisations if, and when I want to do so; I did not feel like doing so on Bastille Day, 1971. In fact, for the last eighteen years I haven't done anything I didn't want to do, and I intend to continue in that way. You are not entitled to lecture me on my duty, Charles, and you shouldn't have called me a prostitute. What would you call someone who writes the sleeve-notes of a record for money, and then reviews the same record for money? (Thank you for all the nice things you said.)

A critic must report the facts: opinion is only worthwhile when it is informed. You have always been kind to me, but you must, as critic (just as I must, as an academic) subordinate kindness and your opinions to the facts.

We can always change our opinions, but facts remain immutable. So, when Doctor Donal O'Sullivan states, as fact, in *The Journal of the Irish Folk Song Society,* Vols XXVIII-XXIX, 1939, p.34, that 'The earliest recorded association of the tune with Limerick' (he is referring to the tune in the Bunting Collection commonly called 'Limerick's Lamentation') 'is in Daniel Wright's Aria Di (*sic*) Camera, published about 1730 ...' he errs, since another version of the tune is in John and

William Neal's collection of the *Most Celebrated Irish Tunes* (Dublin, 1726). Facts, my dear Charles, facts, facts, facts.

Facts, indeed. In *The Irish Times* of September 13th, 1957, you said of my *Nomos No. 1, Hercules Dux Ferrariae*: 'I felt that some of the eight short movements remained little more than ... acrostics.' Yet, in 1970, you were able to describe it as 'a combination of imagination and concentrated, lyrical, musical thought', on the sleeve note of the record. You evidently changed your mind. Twelve years ago, your interest in Irish music was not overwhelming. I delivered a series of fourteen lectures on Radio Éireann, called *Our Musical Heritage*, and the subject became of interest to you. (I still have some of your letters on the subject; I may not answer letters very well or very frequently, but I am a diligent conserver of other people's letters to me). Since then I have been learning, but I'm afraid, my dear Charles, that my opinions of twelve years are still your guide. One of these days I must tell you what I have learned since then. We must learn until we die; we must learn or die.

What have I learned? Very broadly, that there are in this small island two nations: the Irish (or Gaelic) nation, and the Pale. The Irish nation, tiny as it is at the moment, has a long, professional literary and musical tradition. The Pale, on the other hand, has a tradition of amateurishness. (May I remind you of such stuffed owls as the eighteenth-century Pale composers Doctor Philip Cogan, and that poor man the Earl of Mornington, and invite you to have a hearty laugh?).

Three hundred years of this Pale amateurishness are, however, ultimately boring. It has about the same relevance for the Irish nation as would have a column about beekeeping in a tricyclists' monthly journal. Nevertheless, I suppose we should, at least, be grateful for the existence of the Pale; it pays much of our taxes, and occasionally pats us on the head.

One word of advice, my dear Charles: never go into the fortune-telling business. I have in front of me a headline from *The Irish Times* of June 27th, 1960. Again, your good self saying apropos my 'Festival Overture', 'This overture should endure'. How wrong you were! There, there, dear uncle! It was never performed again. In *The Irish Times* of November 2nd, 1959, you said of my *Nomos No. 4 for Piano Concertante and Orchestra* ... 'the best work we have had from an Irish pen.' Alas, another non-starter. It begins to look as if your praise destroys, while your condemnation ... ? Your headline 'Seán Ó Riada one-man show lacked polish' makes me feel a little more encouraged. And who knows, in ten years' time, you may agree with what I believe now; but by then, perhaps, I may have annoyingly changed my mind again (having learned more?).

Dear Charles, you must forget about the Pale. Come to the Gaeltacht, where we still survive, and see and hear the people singing my setting of the mass, in its proper context. As I recall, you thought it was too difficult, too complex for an ordinary congregation. Perhaps it is, for people in the Pale. For us, the remaining Red Indians on the reservation, it presents no problems. Old ladies of 80, children of three or four, born into our tradition, never thought it difficult, for nobody told them so. In the heel of the hunt, you are a foreigner; but you are welcome to become one of the natives, should you wish to do so. There's always an open door here.

One last word – 'amiable' I am not.

Affectionately,

Seán Ó Riada

P.S. Last year, at my UCD concert, you referred to my use of 'Mendelssohnian salon harmony'. Do I take it that Mendelssohnian harmony and salon harmony are identical? If identical, are you not tautologous? If different, where lies the difference? Is it in Mendelssohn's use of the dominant major and minor 9ths (surely a commonplace in 'salon' harmony)? I would like to know, so as to be able to avoid error in future. I have a tape-recording of that concert, as, indeed, of all my other concerts. Should you not be able to remember the precise point at which you discovered 'Mendelssohnian salon harmony', you are, as always, welcome at my house to listen to the tapes and publish your findings afterwards.

As ever,

Seán

A REPLY TO SEÁN Ó RIADA

CHARLES ACTON

My dear Seán,

First of all, may I say how flattered and complimented I feel by your long letter. However passionately a critic feels about the subjects of his opinions, he can, at the best, only hope to be an adjunct and auxiliary to the composers and performers of our art. Therefore, when one whom he regards as having potential genius as a composer publicly calls a critic his friend, let alone a sort of well-meaning uncle, the latter must feel warmly grateful. Even though I am surprised at the implications of seniority.

Now it seems to me that your letter has three basic aspects: – the relationship of critic to performer and composer, accuracy and facts, and what you specifically should be doing with your great talents. Let us deal with the middle one first, partly because it is less important than the other two and partly because you yourself stress these words so strongly in your letter.

To begin with, you are not quite accurate about the function of a critic. You say 'a critic must report the facts: opinion is only worthwhile when it is informed' and 'the critic may voice opinions ... but the facts are of ... paramount importance'. Contrariwise, a critic must express his opinions: that is his first duty and what he is paid for. It is not a critic's first duty to report facts, though occasionally, as in my last notice of you, tentative excursions into reporters' territory are tolerated. I agree with you, however, that opinion is likely to be more valuable and more acceptable if it is well informed. I am a disciple of C.P. Scott about the importance of facts, and, while having no pretensions to being a scholar, I try my best to achieve accuracy. Indeed, only a few weeks ago there was a letter to the Editor objecting to my concern with facts and accuracy. Critics can't win either way perhaps.

Of Mozart's attitude to pianos and harpsichords, may I refer you to Einstein chapter 14, and Sadie's biography page 101.

Of Miss Peg O'Donohue and Miss Gobnait Baróid and so on, you are not quite accurate. I have since learnt that one other trained listener and one professional reporter (at least) received exactly the impression I did. I was listening hard, with even more particular attention than I would try to give you anyway, since you seemed to be leading to a matter of absorbing interest. You would be able to confirm from your tapes what you did say, but would you consider the possibility that my inability as an acting reporter may have been met by less than complete clarity in your exposition? I feel certain that you did use the words 'exactly as she sang it' to you last year, for I wrote them down immediately and as applying to how you were going to play the tune. If I misheard you, I owe my readers and you an apology which I am happy to give. If not, pray avoid the politicians' all-too-frequent claim to have been misreported.

I know that you are extremely busy, but may we ask you to be a little bit more generous of your time in passing on the facts at your disposal. Thus, if the harmonies used by you on July 14th 'had been used ... in the native Irish tradition (a vague expression but we know what you mean) for at least four centuries', i.e., since 1571, it would, I think, interest a great many people to know the evidence for that assertion.

Thanks indeed for your warning against secondary sources of information (though you, like me, have to do so throughout your ordinary life). We have not got a copy of Chappell in *The Irish Times* office, so I had the alternative secondary source of yourself and Percy Scholes. The latter had worldwide renown for punctilious accuracy and repeatedly invited correction of any mis-statement of his. He also wrote a complete book (which I am sure you know) on the history of this one tune. And as a matter of accuracy you did 'show how a song called "Robin is my Delight" was "God Save the Queen".' Demonstration does not have to be expressly verbal, and I think your denial comes close to prevarication.

If Doctor Scholes was also wrong about John Stafford Smith's authorship of the tune of 'Anacreon in Heaven' (which is said also to have been a regimental song of one of the Inniskilling *(sic)* Regiments), you should let the world know. An association between a tune by Carolan (d. 1738) and the Anacreontic Society of London (founded 1766) would be most interesting from a number of points of view.

Doctor Donal O'Sullivan stands far above the need for any defence from me, but surely you are being a little unkind to him about his tune No. 177, which he states 'may not be by Carolan' and which he notes (in Vol II p. 110) he had failed to trace to its source. And would not your Munster generosity and kindness have led you rather to write to Doctor O'Sullivan and give him this information? But may I offer you a new fancy to toy with? 'Judas Maccabaeus' was written in 1747, five years after Handel's visit to Dublin. Handel often used other men's tunes: it is far more plausible that Handel picked up a tune of Carolan's and used it than that the Anacreontics did. But please, if you do use this fancy, do not say that I said he did!

As a matter of strict accuracy, the Church of Ireland does not seem to have been cherishing any tune called 'Athlone' or any tune attributed to Carolan (unfortunately) nor any metrical version of Psalm 60 a mere 138 years after Carolan's death, in the 1876 Church Hymnal.

I am very much flattered that you should retain and refer to my notices of your work. Forgive me therefore for saying that you should know the difference between the future indicative tense and the conditional. Had the words been 'this overture will endure' that would indeed have been prophecy (and extremely rash at that). 'This overture should endure' suggests rather that in the opinion of the writer it ought to if durability were only a matter of its merits. But, as well, you should by now know that headlines in a newspaper are the prerogative of the sub-editors and are not normally written by regular contributors. I was very glad indeed to read that headline, but I certainly did not write it.

Do not be too discouraged because my praise of your piano concertante should have condemned it to silence. Many another good work has had to wait at least as long, and your unrealised intention of playing the slow movement as an isolated piano piece at the Belfast Festival at which you were composer of the year has probably led to a forthcoming request to you to permit its publication.

I am afraid that I do not understand the relevance of your comments 'facts, indeed' in connection with a change in my opinion of your *Hercules* ... (If we are to have facts, my notice appeared on September 14th, 1957 and not on the 13th as you state). My opinion of the work has certainly changed. Why not? But would it not have been more honest, if you are going to quote from a notice now 14 years old, to have included the words 'I certainly (did) not intend to make a final judgment of John Reidy's new serial work having heard only (that) performance?' And that I stressed that my notice was 'first impressions' at 'first hearing'?

Apart from anything else, it is worth recalling that in 1957 you had had plenty of first-hand acquaintance with serialism on the continent, while to many of us in Ireland it was still a technique with which we were only slightly acquainted. You are perfectly right to say that I changed my opinion. I often find cause to. Not only so, but I became sufficiently enthusiastic about the work to bore our mutual friend Garech Browne with pleas that Claddagh Records should record it and, as a (part-time) employee of the Cultural Relations Committee, successfully urged upon them the desirability of assisting its publication.

Since you impugn my integrity by asking 'what would you call someone who writes the sleeve notes of a record for money, and then reviews the same record for money', you might have reassured our readers that I wrote in my review: 'I must, however, declare an inter-est. Claddagh Records had invited me to write the sleeve notes, after enquiring whether I would still feel free to review the record. As I had already heard the pressings and was full of excitement about it, I do not feel debarred, and I would certainly have refused the invitation if I had not thought the record very good.' I see no conflict between writing sleeve notes and reviewing, provided the readers of the review are aware of this and provided there is no conflict between any of the opinions expressed.

As you claim to be an academic in terms of accuracy, please permit me to worry about your sentences: 'Twelve years ago your interest in Irish music was not overwhelming. I delivered a series of 14 lectures on Radio Éireann called *Our Musical Heritage* and the subject became of interest to you.' You know nothing about my interest in Irish music previous to 12 years ago. Long before I was a critic and was only an amateur musician, I was doing what I could to assist the cause of Irish music, especially in respect of Irish composers and performers. But, of course, you mean Irish traditional music, though you ought not to deny Irishness to your *Hercules* or to Seoirse Bodley's symphony, unless you also deny Italianness to Verdi or Germanness to Hindemith.

Of Irish traditional music, I certainly knew even less then than I do now, but my interest was not necessarily any the less and was not primarily aroused by you. Peaks of influence on me go back to the gift of a record of *An túirnín lín* in about 1930, a broadcast of a slow air on the viola in the early 1940s played by the late Tom Collins and other events as long ago as that. The start of some serious acquisition of knowledge (however slight) I owe to Michael and Gráinne Yeats well before your lectures, enormously though the latter interested and stimulated me. I should add that I have often been castigated since for ouch! accepting as accurate various of the contents of your lectures. And I hope you will not be hurt to learn that your opinions of twelve years ago are not still my guide, though I am so very glad to read your 'we must learn until we die: we must learn or die' – and, of course, the more we try to learn the more awed we are by the ever-increasing quantity that we discover remaining to be learnt.

One trouble about the concert notice is the perennial necessity for compression. In writing 'Mendelssohnian salon harmony' rather than expanding it in detail, I hoped that my readers (and you, if you honoured me by reading it) would know what I meant without expansion. I believe that they (and you) did.

Your analysis of our state suggests to me a difference of opinion between us analagous to the difference between the Westernisers and the Panslavophiles in nineteenth-century Russia. And I am avowedly, in that context, a Westerniser. I do not accept that 'Hercules' is foreign, I do not accept that Ireland should be the one country of Europe whose composers cannot contribute to the art of the Western world without being deracinated. Professor Seán Ó Tuama of your own university has investigated the relationship between Munster songs and those of the trouveres. If Ireland was artistically part of Europe in the Middle Ages, why would you cut her off now?

What was wrong with the eighteenth-century worthies was not their association with international music but just that they were not very good. Had Philip Cogan or any of his contemporaries had the genius of Haydn, or even the abilities of Salieri or Berwald, you might not be quite so rude about them. But mention of Philip Cogan brings us to the real crux. It is a pity that my urgings and appeals seem to you as mere admonishments. But I do feel so strongly you have it in you to be a far more considerable composer than Berwald, that I am distressed that you should turn your back on your potentialities.

When you did me the honour of being inteviewed for *Éire-Ireland* I put it to you that 'when I was once singing your praises somebody said "Look, I am fed up with hearing about Seán Ó Riada and his

genius as a composer, when all we've got for it is *Hercules*, a piano concerto and a couple of handfuls of songs. When is he going to produce
more evidence?"' And you asked "What kind of evidence does he want?
... After all, you've got the score of *Hercules* published. You have the
score of my first mass coming out. I hope next year that the *Holderlin
Songs* will be published ... and we have this gramophone record ... isn't
all that evidence?" It was not my job to argue. But now, I would like
to answer your question by saying that if you wrote no more than that,
your total output would be less than that of Duparc, the miracle of
whose life is that he has earned immortality on his sixteen short
'Melodies'. Much as I do admire what work we have from you, I must
now put it bluntly to you that in my opinion (see the beginning of all
this) your catalogue cannot yet stand beside Duparc's. Indeed, *sub
specie aeternitatis*, your output up to date could be compared not too
unreasonably with that of Doctor Philip Cogan, whose work I think
you underrate.

I am well aware that for the last 18 years you haven't done anything
you didn't want to do, and I am even sadder that you intend to continue in that way. Because I still believe that, were you to desire to become
a fully professional composer, you would certainly equal Duparc and
greatly exceed Cogan. But by using the line of least resistance, as I am
afraid you are doing, I feel that you are in grave danger of becoming 'a
man of enormous promise – in the past'. Please don't do that, Seán. And,
returning to your one-man show, it is my sad conviction that it was not
sufficiently polished for a professional entertainer and was a sad waste of
your particular gifts. If you feel that you have been accused of prostitut-
ing those gifts, or, to put it another way, selling part of Ireland's heritage
for a mess of pottage, will you please help us by making sure that such
accusations in the future are totally unfounded?

As a private person you are entitled to do only what you want.
Unfortunately, many people, myself included, believe that you have
talents which are a public responsibility. It is said that when Arthur

Rubinstein was in his fifties and taking life very much as it came, without bothering to keep his talents polished, it came to him: 'Was it to be said of me that I could have been a great pianist? Was this the kind of legacy to leave my wife and children?' And at that he started working hard, with the result that we all admire. Seán, what is to be said of you? Do you really think that that rather amateurish entertainment on Bastille Day was worthy of the great composer you could be? Seán, we admire you, we believe in you, we are honoured to know you, but please accept the burden we put upon you. I write in the plural because I do not speak for myself alone.

And finally, believe me that I write this in deep sincerity and true friendship, and cherishing the privilege of being regarded by you as your friend.

Yours,

Charles Acton

The above is the complete correspondence as it appeared in *The Irish Times*. However, in examining Seán's papers in Cúil Aodha during research for this biography, part of a letter was unearthed, clearly a continuation of the above correspondence. It was scribbled in red ink on an unused examination script of one of his UCC music students, with the student's name still clearly visible.

This certainly never appeared in the columns of *The Irish Times*.

A FRIEND'S REPLY TO A FRIEND'S REPLY TO A FRIEND'S LETTER
I.E. SEÁN Ó RIADA TO CHARLES ACTON TO SEÁN Ó RIADA

My dear Charles,

Lookit here to me – this must stop! Do you realise that you are making me write more letters than I wrote in years? Have you no pity? I have a good mind to telephone you instead, but the difficulties involved in that kind of operation (from both sides) are daunting, to say the least.

12P.

OLLSCOIL NA hÉIREANN
The National University of Ireland

An COLÁISTE OLLSCOILE _Cork_
University College

Do na Scrúduitheoirí amháin	
1	
2	
3	
4	
5	
6	
7	
8	
9	
10	
11	
12	

Uimhir Scrúduithe
Examination Number

345

Ainm an Iarrthóra
Name of Candidate

Bernadette Mc Naughton

Scrúdú } 1sT HATs _Summer 1991_

Examination

Ábhar }
Subject } _Music_

Pas nó Onóracha }
Pass or Honours }

Páipéar {
Paper {   I

Is ceadaithe d'iarrthóirí scríobhadh ar chúl gach leathanaigh den leabhar freagraí seo.
Candidates will be allowed to write on the front and back of each page of this Answer Book.

A Friend's Reply to a Friend's Reply to a friend's Letter;
i.e. Seán Ó Riada to Charles Acton, to Seán Ó Riada

My dear Charles,

Looking here to me — this must stop! Do you
realise that you are making me write more letters than I wrote
in years? Have you no pity? I have a good mind to telephone you
instead, but the difficulties involved in that kind of operation
(from both sides) are daunting, to say the least.

I marvel at the way other people are, or used to be, able to
write letters. James Joyce, now, was a great epistolarian — for the last
two or three nights I have been re-reading his letters in bed. Where
did he find the time for all this _furor [litterarum] scribendi_? Of
course, he didn't produce a great deal of work, only a handful
of books (I suppose you'd describe him as a class of Duparc!)
But then, the books he made he made well; he never yielded to the
dictates of the ephemeral, the fashionable. (Mind you, the ephemeral &
fashionable did their best to imitate him after he had achieved some
success, but, sure, it wasn't the same thing at all).

This question of output is disturbing, just the same. Haydn
could produce 104 symphonies, but then, like Bill's gander, he lived very

Incomplete draft of Seán's final unpublished reply to Charles Acton.

197

I marvel at the way other people are, or used to be, able to write letters. James Joyce, now, was a great epistolarian – for the last two or three nights I have been reading his letters in bed. Where did he find the time for all this furor [*litterari*] scribendi? Of course, he didn't produce a great deal of work, only a handful of books (I suppose you'd describe him as a class of Duparc). But then, the books he made he made well; he never yielded to the dictates of the ephemeral, the fashionable. (Mind you, the ephemeral and fashionable did their best to imitate him after he had achieved some success, but, sure, it wasn't the same thing at all.)

This question of output is disturbing, just the same. Haydn could produce 104 symphonies, but then, like Bill's gander, 'he lived very ...

I was not able to find the rest of what was probably Seán's last letter, since he died soon afterwards.

The correspondence between Ó Riada and Acton sparked a few contributions from other scribes.

David Hanly of Rathfarnham, whose letter appeared on 7 August, had this to say:

Sir, One more word from either Mr Ó Riada or Mr Acton will be a bore, Uncles and nephews shouldn't really pat each other viciously on the head in public. For the record, though, let me say that I also understood Mr Ó Riada to say what Mr Acton thought he said (you understand). I accept Mr Ó Riada's explanation; I am prepared to accept also that the misunderstanding on my part was not due to my bad hearing or Mr Ó Riada's careless delivery. Rather was it a result of being unfortunately seated directly behind the pig-tailed patron Mr Garech Browne and his party, who snickered and whispered and chatted throughout the show. Give that gentleman his due, Mr Browne did several times attempt to persuade his companions that they were at a concert, and not a midnight frolic behind a hedge in Trinity. Bootless.* They would not be quieted. I am all for allowing Mr Browne into these concerts, and God knows I have nothing at all against his charming companions; but should we have to suffer these people at cultural gatherings which impose an (apparently) terrific strain on their minds? - Yours, etc.,

DAVID HANLY,
50 Butterfield Close,
Rathfarnham,
Dublin 14.

*_I have not altered David Hanly's letter, though I feel that 'Bootless' should read 'Fruitless' ... (T.Ó C.)_

A week later, on August 11, Garech de Brun replied:

Sir, I am grateful that thanks to the generosity of your correspondent Mr David Hanly I shall be permitted to continue to listen to Irish music – even with my pigtail. At the same time I must beg Mr Hanly, whom I was not aware of ever having met, not to assume that his own reactions to music are shared by everyone else.

I have no personal experience of the midnight frolics behind the hedges of Trinity that Mr Hanly apparently indulges in (or perhaps only observes?). The fact is that I did not bring the person sitting beside me to the concert. When I saw that she had been moved to tears by Ó Riada's music (as I have been on occasion myself) I gave her my handkerchief.

If to be moved by fine music is a breach of decorum, Mr Hanly at least will not have to plead guilty. Yours, etc.
GARECH de BRUN,
Log a' Lagha,

An Tochar,

Condae Chill Mhanntain.

Less than two months later *The Irish Times* carried the following obituary written by Charles Acton:

OBITUARY

SEÁN Ó RIADA CHANGED SOUND OF IRISH TRADITIONAL MUSIC

CHARLES ACTON

Seán Ó Riada, the composer and musician, who died yesterday in a London hospital, was born in Cork on August 1st, 1931. His father's family came from Co. Clare, where his great-grandfather was part farmer, part sculptor, part poet, and translated the *Odyssey* into Irish.

His mother's is a Cork family and stems from the Mac Criddans whose names are on the Dalway harp. He was educated by the Christian Brothers at Adare, Co. Limerick, and at UCC where he read classics and music, graduating in 1952, and studied the piano and harmony under Aloys G. Fleischmann, senior, whose death called forth the beautiful song cycle of 1964, *In Memoriam Aloys Fleischmann,* to poems by Hölderlin.

On graduating he became assistant director of music in Radio Éireann, a position he relinquished soon in order to study in Paris and Italy. In Paris, he came under the influence of Florent Schmidt and Olivier Messiaen (to be simultaneously influenced by both is surely strange?) and had the opportunity of appearing as a pianist, playing music of his own, since withdrawn, in two quarter-hour programmes of *Soloistes Internationaux* on Paris Radio in 1954. It was in this period that he met serialism and felt that it was more akin to the melodic and decorative ideas of traditional Irish music than the classically formed music of his formal education.

After returning to Ireland, he became director of music for the Abbey Theatre (in the Queen's), where he learnt much of the ordinary practical techniques that he used in his film music and with his group of musicians. He sprang into nationwide prominence with his brilliant music for George Morrison's film *Mise Éire*, made for Gael-Linn, where, among other things, he showed that there was more depth in the tune of *Róisín Dubh* than most of his compatriots had ever realised and brought many of them to take a new pride in their musical heritage.

At the opening of the 1961 Dublin Theatre Festival, Seán Ó Riada unveiled his Ceoltóirí Chualann, his new type of band. The Clandillon type of ceili band had been battering the life out of Irish dance music for more than 30 years. Ó Riada was about the only man capable of diverting popular enjoyment of ceili (and other traditional) music into new (or more traditional) directions. In theory it was to have a wide variety of unison timbres with jazz-type opportunities for stretches of virtuoso solo variation and with creative arrangements of traditional music and perhaps actual composition, using in the new-old form ancient techniques such as canon, canon with augmentation and other contrapuntal means, leading to a new synthesis of age-old Irish tradition and European means. Though these theoretical hopes were never fully realised for a variety of reasons which may have led to their disbandment as such in 1970, they had a nationwide (and larger) popularity that has changed the ceili picture and generated successors such as The Chieftains.

At that time, O Riada was living in a Georgian house in Galloping Green (and driving an ancient and capacious Jaguar), where his living-room was deliberately uncarpeted for the sake of the frequent sessions of traditional dancing and music-making which were as famous and signficant as any meetings of the old Pipers' Club.

After the late Seán Neeson's retirement, Seán Ó Riada was appointed Cork Corporation lecturer in music in University College Cork, and soon took up residence in Cúil Aodha, in the west Cork Gaeltacht, whence he commuted to Cork; to emerge for broadcasts and live performances and Gael Linn recordings by his Ceoltóirí; to write music in this genre for, among other films, that of *The Playboy of the Western World*; to be music adviser for Gael-Linn's recordings; to be the 1967 Belfast Festival's composer of the year; or to divert himself and his family on a Galway hooker in the Kenmare River.

Life as a member of the Irish-speaking rural community at Cúil Aodha and the post-Vatican liberation of liturgical music led to his setting of the mass, in the idiom of traditional Irish music, for Cúil Aodha parish, which has since been used in many places; and of a second setting last year commissioned by Glenstal Abbey.

As a result of the tercentenary commemorations of Carolan in Cork last year, he founded the Carolan Society which he hoped would have an important future for traditional music in Ireland and in the United States of America. Also last year, Claddagh Records issued their *Vertical Man*, the first issue by an Irish commercial gramophone record company of a record of art music by any Irish composer.

He is survived by his wife Ruth and seven children.

As a composer Seán Ó Riada had immense promise to be, possibly, our first great composer. The width of his activity, his zest for actual life threatened the realisation of this promise, a continued anxiety to many of his friends. His life having been so tragically cut short in his prime, this promise cannot now be fulfilled. His actual catalogue is tiny, smaller even than that of Henri Duparc. His *Olynthiac Overture*, a sparkling example of a classically diatonic orchestral composition, deserves as firm a place in the Irish orchestral repertoire as, say, that of *The Bartered Bride*. His *Hercules Dux Ferrariae*, in spite of a few signs of technical inexperience, is a work of excitement and beauty of which we should remain proud for many years. His piano concerto badly needs reviving. His Hölderlin songs, though of a simplicity that has baffled avant-garde Europeans, has a beauty comparable with the equally individual songs of Kilpinen. He is perhaps the only Irish composer that the ordinary concert-goer could listen to for a complete concert – and be as completely satisfied as the modern music devotee. Apart from his few compositions, he was justified in claiming to have changed the sound of traditional music in Ireland. No-one can forget the impact his Mise Éire music made on his country. Whatever their merits, his settings of the mass should lead to a new national vision of liturgical music.

Whatever the long-term survival of his compositions, he had a profound influence in many parts of Irish musical life. It may be that his zest for life, the variety of his activities, his sense of wit and paradox, the remarkable width of his friendships, the impact of his conversation and thought, may have diluted his concrete, visible achievements: but the intensely imaginative way in which he went through life showed that, in a very real way, his life itself was a process of artistic, imaginative creation, though he would never have thought of it in that way. Let us hope that many of the ideas which he flung out so enthusiastically may be taken up and used now that he has gone.

It is known that an important organisation had commissioned from him a commemorative work to be used after the death of a very famous citizen. Let us hope that it was completed and that it is worthy of the subject and the composer, and that it may now be used to commemorate the first composer essentially of modern Ireland to be taken from us.

APPENDIX II

MUSIC BY SEÁN Ó RIADA: SOURCES

GAEL LINN
CDs:
Reacaireacht an Riadaigh: CEFCD 010
Ceol na n-uasal: CEFCD 015
Ding Dong: CEFCD 016
Ó Riada sa Gaiety: CEFCD 027
Ó Riada: CEFCD 032
Mise Éire: CEFCD 080

VIDEOS:
Mise Éire
Saoirse

TAPES:
Ceol An Aifrinn (Music of the Mass)

CLADDAGH RECORDS
Ó Riada's Farewell CC12CD

Scores and recordings of Seán Ó Riada's orchestral compostions are available in the RTÉ Music Library.

BIBLIOGRAPHY

note the order [sic]

Seán Ó Riada: *Nomos No. 1: Hercules Dux Ferrariae.* Woodtown

Seán Ó Riada: *Aifreann 1*

Seán Ó Riada: *Aifreann 2*

Seán Ó Riada: Evaluating Schoenberg. B. Mus. thesis, UCC, 1952.

Seán Ó Riada: eds. T. Kinsella and T. Ó Canainn. *Our Musical Heritage.* Dolmen 1982.

Seán Ó Riada: *Ceist-freagra.* Comhar, Lúnasa, 1964.

Seán Ó Riada: *Ceol agus Ól.* Comhar, Eanáir, 1961.

Seán Ó Riada: *An dá chuileat.* Comhar, Bealtaine 1961.

Seán Ó Riada: *An feall. Comhar,* Aibreán, 1969.

Seán Ó Riada: *Máirtín Ó Cadhain.* Samhain, 1970.

Seán Ó Riada: *Ag labhairt le Nollaig Ó Gadhra.* Comhar 1965, reprinted Deireadh Fómhair 1991.

T Ó Canainn and G. Mac an Bhua: *Seán Ó Riada: a Shaol agus a Shaothar.* Gartán 1993.

T. Ó Canainn: *A Lifetime of Notes.* The Collins Press 1996.

T.Ó Canainn: *Seán Ó Riada, an Léachtóir.* Comhar, Márta 1972.

T.Ó Canainn: *Seán Ó Riada. Cork Examiner,* October 3, 1991.

T. Ó Canainn: *Seán Binn an Cheoil.* Feasta, Deireadh Fómhair 1991.

T.Ó Canainn: *Seán Ó Riada. Sunday Independent,* March 1, 1998.

T.Ó Canainn: *Oidhreacht an Riadaigh. Foinse,* Meán Fómhair 30, 2001.

G. Victory: *The World of Ó Riada. Written on the Wind: Personal Memories of Irish Radio.* 1976.

B. Harris and G. Freyer, editors: *The Achievement of Seán Ó Riada.* Irish Humanities Centre & Keohanes: 1981.

A. Fleischmann: Seán Ó Riada, *Counterpoint,* November 1971.

A. Fleischmann: Seán Ó Riada's Nomos No.2, *Éire-Ireland,* 1972.

Treasa O'Driscoll: *In the Deep Heart's Core: An Irishwoman's Soul Journey.* Kyrios Press, Alabaster, Ala, USA, 2000

Nollaig Ó Gadhra: He secured Irish music's future. *Cork Examiner,* October 3, 1991.

Conchúr Ó Tuama: *Seán Ó Riada agus an Ceol Dúchasach.* Comhar, Márta 1972.

P. Ó Dubháin: An Ghné Chlasaiceach. *Comhar,* Márta 1972.

Seán Ó Muineacháin: *Seán Ó Riada, Gael Uasal.* Treoir, November/December 1971.

Tim Danaher: He was of Ireland and the Irish. *Treoir,* November/December 1971.

An Mangaire Súgach: *Prayers, Music and Tears.* Treoir, November/December 1971.

Riobárd Mac Góráin: *Seán Ó Riada. Feasta,* Deireadh Fómhair 1991.

Charles Acton: Seán Ó Riada: The Next Phase, *Éire-Ireland,* 1967.

Charles Acton: Interview with Seán Ó Riada: *Éire-Ireland,* Spring 1971.

Charles Acton: I gCuimhne Sheáin Uí Riada. *Éire-Ireland,* Winter 1971.

Donncha Ó Cróinín: *Maranadh ar an Riadach. Feasta,* Deireadh Fómhair 1991.

Seán Ua Cearnaigh: *Caoineadh Sheáin Uí Riada,* Feasta, Deireadh Fómhair 1991.

Charles Acton: *Éifeacht Sheáin Ui Riada.* Feasta, Deireadh Fómhair 1991.

Seán Ó Sé: *Mise agus Seán Ó Riada.* Feasta, Deireadh Fómhair 1991.

Peadar Ó Riada: *M'Athair. Feasta,* Deireadh Fómhair 1991.

E. Deale: *A Catalogue of Contemporary Irish Composers,* Dublin, 1973.

H. White: 'Music and the Irish Literary Imagination', *Irish Musical Studies* III, 1995

H. White: *The Keeper's Recital: Music and Cultural History in Ireland 1770-1970.*

D. Breathnach and M. Ní Mhurchú: *Beathaisnéis A Cúig.* An Clóchomhar. 1997

R. Deane: Ó Riada is dead - Long Live Ó Riada. *The Journal of Music in Ireland.* January/February 2001.

Seoirse Bodley: Remembering Seán Ó Riada. *Capuchin Annual.* 1972.

Oliver Sweeney: The Ó Riada Legacy. *Hot Press.* 4 June 1987.

Seán Ó Mórdha: Seán Ó Riada. *The Irish Times,* 20 April 1987.

Gerard O'Grady: An appreciation of Sean Ó Riada. *Folk Review.* July 1972.

INDEX